POWER ON THE BACK BENCHES?
The growth of select committee influence

Derek Hawes

S·A·U·S

First published in Great Britain in 1993 by

SAUS Publications
School for Advanced Urban Studies
University of Bristol
Rodney Lodge
Grange Road
Bristol BS8 4EA

Telephone (0272) 741117
Fax (0272) 737308

© SAUS 1993

British Library Cataloguing in Publication Data
A catalogue record for this book is available from the British Library

SAUS Study 10

ISBN   1 873575 42 4
ISSN   0268-3725

The School for Advanced Urban Studies is a centre for research, post-graduate and continuing education, and consultancy at the University of Bristol.   The School's focus is the analysis, development and implementation of policy in the fields of employment, health and social care, housing, social management, and urban change and government. Its aim is to bridge the gaps between theory and practice, between different policy areas, and between academic disciplines. SAUS is committed to the wide dissemination of its findings and in addition to courses and seminars the School has established several publications series: **SAUS Studies, Occasional Papers, Working Papers, Studies in Decentralisation and Quasi-Markets, DRIC Reports and SAUS Guides and Reports.**

SAUS is working to counter discrimination on grounds of gender, race, disability, age and sexuality in all its activities.

Printed in Great Britain by The Alden Press, Oxford, OX2 0EF.

CONTENTS

LIST OF FIGURES

LIST OF TABLES

LIST OF ABBREVIATIONS

BNFL	British Nuclear Fuels Ltd
CBI	Confederation of British Industry
CEC	Commission of the European Communities
CEGB	Central Electricity Generating Board
CFC	Chlorofluorocarbons
CIA	Chemical Industries Association
CPRE	Council for the Protection of Rural England
CPRS	Central Policy Review Staff
DHSS	Department of Health and Social Security
DOE	Department of the Environment
DTI	Department of Trade and Industry
EC	European Community
FGD	Flue-gas desulphurisation
FMI	Financial Management Initiative
GLC	Greater London Council
HATs	Housing action trusts
HBF	House Builders Federation
MAFF	Ministry of Agriculture, Fisheries and Food
MINIS	Management Information System for Ministers
NAO	National Audit Office
NCB	National Coal Board
NCC	Nature Conservancy Council
NEDO	National Economic Development Organisation
NFU	National Farmers Union
NIREX	Nuclear Industry Radioactive Waste Executive
PAC	Public Accounts Committee
PSA	Property Services Agency
RSPB	Royal Society for the Protection of Birds
RTPI	Royal Town Planning Institute
TUC	Trades Union Congress
UDCs	Urban development corporations
WDA	Waste Disposal Authority

ACKNOWLEDGEMENTS

This book derives from a larger academic thesis undertaken at the School for Advanced Urban Studies, University of Bristol, the completion of which was assisted considerably by the cooperation of numerous officers and members of the House of Commons and many other participants in the select committee investigative process. The contribution of witnesses, advisers and commentators is gratefully acknowledged.

The presentation of this work in published form is due largely to the encouragement of academic colleagues and especially Colin Fudge, and Professors Michael Hill and Alan Murie. Particular and affectionate thanks, however, are due to two individuals: Randall Smith whose ever-present support and wise counsel were a constant inspiration, and to Lilian Read whose patience and skill in the preparation of numerous drafts of the original text were essential to its production.

Illustrations and diagrams are by Robin Hawes.

PREFACE

The outcome of the general election of April 1992 was more decisive than most commentators expected, providing the Conservatives with a small but comfortable working majority for a five-year term. Like its predecessor in 1987, the pre-election debate had centred upon serious talk of three-party government, coalition or minority administration, leading to consideration of larger constitutional issues and the way in which those without formal executive power might deploy their new-found influence if the traditional two-party mould should be broken.

In a contribution to that debate Ian Marsh's book, *Policy making in a three-party system* (1986), argued that with power finely balanced between three major parties, the position of the then relatively new parliamentary select committees would inevitably be enhanced, giving them a positive role in policy making. They would take on a deliberative function in the legislative process, have the power to challenge the Executive and become the "catalysts for reconciling interest groups" (Marsh, 1986). He saw the new select committees as a means of institutionalising power-sharing in a multi-party parliament.

As it turned out, Margaret Thatcher's 1987 majority was larger than any in recent history, leading, in the view of many, to a centralising and dictatorial use of power which paid little heed either to opposition or to back-bench opinion.

By contrast to the scenario envisaged by Marsh, this book argues that in fact select committees developed an unexpected constitutional importance as a counterpoint: a platform for the expression of back-bench views, often of a bi-partisan kind which provided, however minimally, an antidote to the overweening centralism and arbitrary use of executive power which many observers felt were the hallmarks of Margaret Thatcher's later prime ministership.

As the departmentally related committee system moves into its fourth parliamentary term, and with the benefit of a thoroughly researched review of progress published by the Commons Procedure Committee covering the first ten years (HC 19, 1990), the role which it establishes for itself may be different again from those of earlier parliaments.

We can be sure, though, that in the process of monitoring each of the departments of state, examining civil servants and quizzing ministers, committee members will seek to ensure their scrutiny leads to influence on policy outcomes and the modification of governmental approaches to the questions of the day. Policy making for back benchers could indeed move nearer to reality as the maturing committee system establishes its credentials in the altogether less hostile and more finely-balanced context of the parliament elected in 1992 and beyond.

The prime purpose of this book is to examine, not so much the influence which committees have demonstrated they can bring to bear, but the ways in which such influence can be measured and the strengths and weaknesses of methodological approaches to this measurement.

INTRODUCTION

The historic struggle of the British Parliament to shake off the dominance of feudal barons, autocratic monarchs, and an all-powerful House of Lords is the long backdrop to this study. Since the time of Edward III, parliament has fought to maintain the principle that it would vote to approve the Monarch's taxes only in return for the redress of grievances: an unremitting claim which needed reinforcing with the Stuarts and Hanoverians, until the great 19th century Reform Bills displaced the hegemony of Crown patronage and successive Whig and Tory oligarchies.

In modern times the context for that struggle has been the House of Commons and in particular the attempts of back-bench members of parliament (MPs) to influence and control the Government of the day. Throughout the 20th century the criticism has been that parliament's role is diminished by the dominance of the Executive; that policy is made elsewhere and that the ability of back-bench MPs to scrutinise the actions of the Government is minimal. From time to time the focus changes: the power of civil servants; the corporatist collaboration between ministers and powerful agencies outside parliament; the power of Government patronage and the autocratic actions of prime ministers, all in one way or another contribute to the frustration of back benchers in their attempts to influence what is summed up in Lord Hailsham's powerful aphorism as the tyranny of "an elective dictatorship" (Hailsham, 1976).

The particular subject of this study is the new system of select committees introduced in 1979, foreshadowed in the 1978 Procedure Committee report, which was parliament's own way of addressing these questions of dominance, influence and power within the political system (HC 558, 1978).

The discussion links to a number of other current debates including the process of policy making in an increasingly technological age and the influence of pressure groups and their access to MPs. The growth of interest in the way in which policy is formed is relevant to the understanding of select committee activity and the intention is to glimpse inside the ubiquitous 'black box' of policy-making theory and to throw light on some of the mechanisms within (Easton, 1965).

The choice of environmental policy as the area upon which to validate the ideas developed was made because it encompasses interests wider than one department of state, touches upon both commercial and industrial activity, and produces interest group response at every level of British society. Primarily, however, it is because it enables some insight to be gained into a particular set of policies which have grown within a decade from peripheral concern to an explosion of public debate at the top of the political agenda. In this book the participation of select committees in that development is assessed and a systematic method of measuring their success is established. The mercurial nature of what constitutes 'success' in this context, and for whom, allows us to examine the multiplicity of ways in which policy and policy makers can be influenced.

The discussion raises a number of issues concerning the future development of the system: the reluctance of back benchers to engage with the monitoring of financial estimates; the limitations placed upon committee powers to question ministers; and the balance between the committee corridor and the floor of the House of Commons in terms of the right theatre for challenging the Government.

All of these issues have been highlighted in the period covered by this book. The Westland Helicopter issue and the refusal of senior civil servants to answer Defence Committee questions have been examples of tensions which occur when select committees touch the more sensitive nerves of the power of the Executive (Drewry, 1987; HC 62, 1986; HC 100, 1986; CM78, 1987).

Power and influence in this context are therefore essentially related to policy and how it is made. If back-bench parliamentarians are concerned to exert more power over policy making they are equally concerned to scrutinise the exercise of policy and the power which is inherent in it.

It has, therefore, been pertinent to conduct much of the discussion in terms of theoretical models of the policy process; to find a conceptual model which enables select committee activity to be understood in terms of its impact on policy, whether in its formation, its application, its evaluation or indeed in its termination and replacement.

A number of approaches to this problem are discussed. Some models have traditionally been used to describe what occurs, others to set normative ground rules for what ought to occur. The contrasting approaches of Simon (1958) and Lindblom (1959; 1980), the debate between rationality and incrementalism, and the attempts of Etzioni (1964) and Dror (1973) to synthesise these approaches are all examined for their relevance to the subject under discussion. They are ultimately rejected as insufficiently helpful in understanding or explaining the role of the back-bench committee in the pluralist environment of Westminster and Whitehall. They fail to deal with the essentially serial nature of policy making which comes back to problems, corrects mistakes, opens up new directions or adapts to new advances in technology. Nor do they sufficiently explicate the psychological subtleties of political debate - bargaining for electoral advantage, or indeed the frequent need for consensus - out of which public policy emerges to be implemented through a constellation of agencies in both public and private contexts.

The need for theoretical validity within this part of the argument, therefore, has led to the requirement for a model which can cope with the complexity of the parliamentary process, which is capable of explaining both rational and incremental policy advance, and describes as well as offers a prescriptive approach to the select committee enthusiast. That is to say, a model that is concerned with the application of techniques and with the political process.

The theoretical underpinning of the central hypothesis, therefore, needs to emphasise the political nature of the policy process, the subjectivity of much analysis and the need to be concerned with the consumption as well as the production of policy advice. It is provided by utilising the work of Hogwood and Gunn (1984) on policy analysis and Easton's (1965) theory of the political system. Both of these models are adapted to the examination of select committee activity in order to provide a conceptual basis for establishing both the role they play within the political system and the function of policy intervention which they perform.

Out of the discussion arise a number of ideas which engage with the ongoing debate about the need for constitutional change in a world in which the speed of political and technological change has reached a state almost of permanent revolution and in which valued institutions must, it seems, change too or become redundant.

Methodology

The methodology employed in pursuing the argument has been to provide a narrative account of the evolution of select committees particularly since the Crossman reforms of the 1960s, and to trace their development through subsequent decades up to the introduction of the present system.

Care has been taken to contrast the assessment of parliamentarians active in the committee system with academic and other outside observers as well as the forecasts of the minority of political activists who viewed the new system as a threat to parliamentary integrity.

By adapting Easton's (1965) 'black box' model of the political system, it can be demonstrated that if the committee system is conceptualised as a miniature version of Easton's model, the process of inputs, outputs and outcomes allows a new approach to be devised for the systematic measurement of effectiveness. An approach to measurement of committee effectiveness is then devised which is two-fold:

(i)   the research undertakes detailed assembly of both the inputs and the outputs of particular committee reports, consisting of a count of all documents, witnesses, technical appendices, memoranda and unpublished evidence together with a count of the citations of such evidence and references made to it in the text of the committee's final report;

(ii)   a triangulation is then attempted of the key factors in the investigative process. Three variables are identified within the committee enquiry: the point within the life-cycle of a policy at which the committee seeks to intervene (intervention), the approach or mode of the committee in pursuing the investigation (committee mode), and the subject matter of particular topics (issue type).

The underlying assumption in constructing this approach to committee impact on policy formulation or change has been that what committees do and how they set about doing it is closely allied to the activities of policy analysts and might best be understood if examined in those terms. At best, committees contribute in a secondary role to original analysis by the Government and its agencies. They expose analysis to critical appraisal in a way which can itself be of analytical value.

It is argued that even after a policy option has been chosen, the role of policy analysis is far from over. It is seen as supplementing the more overtly political aspects of the policy process rather than replacing them, and indeed in an ideal world, as providing the synthesis between politics and analysis which theorists such as those whose work is utilised here have long sought.

The three key factors in the investigative process

● Intervention

It is argued that a crucial factor in the effectiveness of select committee reports is the point in the life-cycle of a policy at which an enquiry is launched. If the committee intervention is at the policy formation stage, or when options are being considered, is it likely to have more impact than if the policy is already well into the implementatio phase? To pursue this point a cyclical model of the policy process is utilised, illustrating that outcomes differ depending upon the point of intervention in particular cases.

● Committee 'mode'

The idea of 'committee mode' to describe approaches adopted in particular investigations allows some differentiation to be made between the purposes of particular committees and particular enquiries. It is established that the purposes of committee members may differ in that they may be wishing to influence a department, or another public sector agency, or indeed to inform MPs for a forthcoming debate. The examples used demonstrate that these variations in goals or purposes are an important ingredient in determining the mode of an enquiry.

● Issue type

A key factor identified in committee enquiries is the nature of the topic which forms the subject of the investigation. In the committee reports under review three such issue types are identified: technical/scientific, economic, and administrative. These three types are described and based upon the main characteristics of the subject matter of individual investigations. Account is taken of the main thrust of the arguments, the nature of the evidence presented and the policy context within which the committee is pursuing its purposes.

Having identified the three key factors in committee investigations, which, it is suggested, have a bearing on effectiveness, a form of triangulation is achieved by the establishment of a matrix which allows each of the three factors to be used as variables in the assessment of committee effectiveness. The strengths and weaknesses of this device are examined in later chapters. The 'best' result in terms of outputs and outcomes begs the question 'best for whom?': an issue pursued in later chapters.

The hypothesis, the validity of the argument developed and the concepts employed are tested against a series of ten select committee reports produced during the parliament of 1983-87, three of which are used as case studies. All of the reports relate to environmental issues and include the work of the Committee for Welsh Affairs, the Trade and Industry Committee as well as the Environment Committee. This area of policy was chosen to provide a limited and consistent body of policy making and political debate within which to work through the ideas propounded.

The primary concern, however, has been to consider how far the new select committee system is effective in giving voice to parliament and back-bench parliamentarians in their struggle to influence, monitor and scrutinise the dominant Executive. By using the language and techniques of policy analysis a taxonomy of influence is evolved which emphasises the multiplicity of means of policy change and development.

The latter part of the book is concerned to analyse the results of the matrix test, and the other procedures described above, and to develop a discussion of the outcome and of alternative means of evaluating committee performance. The value of the matrix in this process, its validity and flaws as a research tool form part of this discussion.

Finally the book makes some recommendations and prescriptive suggestions for the greater effectiveness of select committees, their place both in theoretical terms and in practice within the British democratic state, and the possibilities for an expanded role for select committees within constitutional changes currently being debated.

one

SPECIALIST COMMITTEES FROM CROSSMAN TO ST JOHN STEVAS

The progress of the departmental select committees which arose from the 1979 parliamentary reforms was watched critically throughout the first Thatcher administration of 1979-83. Both political actors and academic commentators sought to evaluate the committees' success and effectiveness and to measure them against the claims which were made for them by the Procedure Committee which recommended the system, and in the debate in the House which set them up.

The contrast between the two perspectives is stark. Even allowing for the perhaps more detached view of outside observers, and a degree of cynicism from long-time commentators on the Westminster scene, the assessment of the value of select committees in monitoring departments of state ranges from the enthusiastic to the pessimistic.

The background

In reviewing the literature on the 1979 reforms it is necessary to put the matter into historical context and to demonstrate that criticism of the diminished role of parliament and of the dominance of the Executive has been a recurring theme throughout the past 50 years. Distinguished commentators from a wide political spectrum have argued for reform since the publication of Harold Laski's *A grammar of politics* warned of the strength of the civil service and the Executive combined (Laski, 1920). Sidney and Beatrice Webb produced *Constitution for the socialist commonwealth* arguing for a radical democratisation of parliament at the same time (Webb and Webb, 1920). Each from different perspectives argued for more power to the House of Commons at the expense of the Executive. Later, Leo Amery in *Thoughts on the constitution* and Winston Churchill in his Romanes lectures examined the possibility of a society in which the major producing groups of unions and employers acquire a political role with important implications for our parliamentary system (Churchill, 1930; Amery, 1951).

Against this long background of complaints about the lack of a proper role for parliament, the modern movement for reform was led throughout the 1960s by prominent parliamentarians supported outside Westminster by the formation of the Study of Parliament Group which has been an active catalyst for change. Two particularly influential studies appeared in the mid 1960s. Bernard Crick's *The reform of parliament* reflected the views of both academics such as Professors Hanson and Wiseman and MPs such as John Mackintosh and Richard Crossman. It was essentially a view from the left which envisaged parliamentary committees as the bridge between informed opinion in the country, interest groups and the Executive. It propounded the idea of a system of pre-legislation committees which would examine Bills before they were presented to the House of Commons (Crick, 1965).

The quite different range of concerns from the right of the political spectrum is expressed in a 1964 publication by Hill and Whichelow concerning itself particularly with parliament's responsibility for controlling and checking public expenditure: "the historic roots of parliament lie very simply in money - the control of the nation's money is at the heart of our parliamentary system". This volume traced the development of parliament's powers to control supply through a series of struggles between the Commons and the Monarch (and later with the Lords), in which the Commons emerged victorious in the control of expenditure.

Crick (1965) is less prescriptive: "control means influence, not direct power; advice not command; criticism not obstruction; scrutiny not initiation". He argues that the only parliamentary controls worth considering are those which do not threaten the parliamentary defeat of a Government but which help to keep it responsive to the underlying currents and the more important drift of public opinion. Hill and Whichelow have to admit that having won the struggle to control supply, the Commons rapidly became an ineffectual mechanism in reality, having rejected estimates of the Executive on only one or two occasions since the First World War.

Thus the twin thrusts of the parliamentary reform movement in the 1960s were the restoration of parliament's historic role in the scrutiny of public expenditure and enhanced public involvement in policy making - but not in a context that would actually threaten the power of the Executive. The emphasis was upon an enlarged role for parliament which could be reconciled with unchanged Executive prerogatives. But nowhere is there an awareness of the difficulty of reconciling the contradictory aims of strong, single-party Government with bi-partisan investigatory powers for the House of Commons.

The Crossman era

In the event the real progenitor of the modern select committee reforms is Richard Crossman whose initiatives in 1966 as lord president of the council established the idea of permanent scrutiny of the deeds of the Government. Ironically it is during this very period that perhaps more extra-parliamentary policy mediation went on than at any other stage in post-war times. It is the period during which there had been a growth in status of corporate agencies particularly in the economic sphere, and a tendency for policy to emerge through a process of collaboration with producer groups and with labour interests which did not only reduce the role of parliament, but subordinated the importance of primary legislation.

The formation of the National Economic Development Organisation (NEDO) in 1962 and the promotion of bodies such as the Trades Union Congress (TUC) and the Confederation of British Industry (CBI) to the centre of the policy process in the technocratic state was supported by many parliamentarians themselves who urged a measure of institutional reform so that collaboration between industry and parliament would forge new processes of economic planning. Middlemass characterised these interest groups as "governing institutions", existing thereafter as estates of the realm committed to cooperation with the state, whilst retaining their customary independence (Middlemass, 1979). This "corporate bias" in the policy-making process accentuated the decline of party and parliamentary politics, and specifically the role of MPs and the Commons. In Winkler's terms the process evolved as a full scale corporatist structure of government with a more directive role for the state in the national politico/economic organisation. It was a distinct and firmly articulated form of corporatism under which the state intensively channelled private business towards the four goals of order, unity, nationalism and success (Winkler, 1974).

Winkler saw the process as a reaction to the economic crisis of the early 1970s and a revulsion against the market processes with the substitution of cooperation for competition and the elevation of the general welfare over self-interest and profit. Thus we have the paradox that the birth of the committee scrutiny system in 1966 came at a moment when the policy process was moving away from the floor of the House of Commons to Downing Street and Whitehall to an unprecedented extent.

It is this contradictory picture which leads Professor Stuart Walkland to a pessimistic appraisal of the developing scene written in 1976 when he concluded that enhanced scrutiny and unchanged Executive prerogatives were incompatible. He judged that effective committee work would be thwarted without the power to challenge the Executive and pointed out that a really successful all-party scrutiny committee would:

> entail a distancing of the House of Commons from the Executive and a diminution in the powers of ministers and party leaders which could only ensue from important alterations in the political structure of parliament and consequent changes in the conventions which govern its relations with the Executive. (Walkland, 1976)

In evidence to a Procedure Committee enquiry in 1977 the Study of Parliament Group reflects the lack of unanimity of the time:

> There are now two main schools of thought. The one that has been dominant this century, perhaps even since 1868 accepts that the power of the Government, derived from the authority it gains from the sanction of a popular franchise and exercised through the party majority in the House, has effectively deprived the House of any direct power of decision making it may ever had had. The Government (ministers plus civil service) governs, and the Government controls the House not vice-versa in any meaningful sense.
>
> There is now emerging a second school of thought which argues that without some measure of power the House of Commons can have no authority; but any power the House

has possessed has been so sapped and eroded by Government that it is now meaningless to talk of parliamentary government in Britain. There are still doubts among some members of the Study of Parliament Group as to whether the largely adversary party situation in the present House of Commons is not basically hostile to an expansion of select committee work and whether a different political structure is not needed to allow select committees to realise the potential they undoubtedly have. (HC 588, 1978)

If these concerns had been caused by the increasing tendency of Labour Governments of the period to mediate policy with extra-parliamentary forces, over beer and sandwiches at No 10, they led other, less polite commentators to describe the tendency in starker terms. An editorial in *The Economist* in 1977 describes what it sees as the tyranny of:

an unparliamentary government that is Britain's lot today. ... As Britain's Executive has done more, as its involvement in economic life has grown and its impact on citizens' powers and freedoms has widened, the capacity of the House of Commons to investigate its activities has diminished. Students of parliamentary institutions all over the world accept that this kind of scrutiny for keeping officials alert and accountable is as effective as its system of regular committees. (*The Economist*, 1977)

The Economist's blueprint for a different political democracy envisages a central parliament which would distance itself from ministers and would have a legislative role, taking on much of the power over the Executive enjoyed by America's congress:

Such a parliament's deliberation would be respected, its speakers admired, its investigative committees heard and its powers ensured by the ancient weapon of the control of the purse and the modern one of televising, in full or edited versions, its sessions both on the floor and in committee.

A review of performance

In a detailed examination of the reports produced by select committees between 1966 and 1969, Shell traces the development of their investigative activities and their impact on ministers and policies. He concludes that they achieved only the most minor influence on policy making and administration and suggests their chief role was to provoke discussion and provide information (Shell, 1970).

The picture painted is one of a struggle for survival against a Government which seemed to see select committees primarily as a useful means of occupying the energies of some of its back benchers. The first of the Crossman committees were established mainly because of the willingness of the appropriate minister to tolerate their presence. Not that this deterred Mr Crossman; according to one colleague:

> in discussion with Labour MPs interested in parliamentary reform he explained that he hoped to set up two more of these departmental committees each year until all domestic policy was subject to scrutiny and the last and most difficult hurdle was reached, the creation of foreign affairs and defence committees. (Mackintosh, 1969)

Shell demonstrates that despite powers to examine papers and persons, these early forerunners of the present committees could do little to respond if faced with a refusal to bow to their requests by government departments or ministers. Despite the proclamation by one committee chair that: "it is definitely our business to attempt to help in the formulation of public policy", a consideration of the fate of recommendations made by the committee would suggest that little has been achieved in that direction. The same chair was later to agree that the minister had "largely ignored" his recommendations (Palmer, 1968).

By the end of the 1969/70 session the select committees were still being referred to as experimental. One cannot help feeling there was an implied threat in the use of that word; if any committee became obstinate or awkward (or, as Shell suggests, simply effective), it was liable not to get reappointed. In this sense the system was unsatisfactory. Shell sums up, rather pessimistically at this stage in the reform process, that although the House could be said to be "slightly better informed" the committees had not been notably successful at digging out facts that the Government had not wished to reveal. The Agriculture Committee which had set out to do this did not succeed and its enthusiasm was rewarded by its disbandment. Nor is there any evidence that the possession of information was equated with the ability to influence policy.

Walkland's view, reviewing the scene a decade after the introduction of the Crossman reforms, is that later leaders of the House were more concerned with efficiency of legislation than added scrutiny, and that select committees were more to do with compensations for back benchers than with a genuine enthusiasm for reform (Walkland, 1976). He opines that the centre of political gravity would shift further to Whitehall from Westminster than it already had in the mid 1970s and that public participation in parliamentary processes would be even more minimal than it already was.

Walkland argued that the 1966 reforms had made little impact upon the main determinants of British parliamentary government and by any test could be said to have failed. Nevertheless there had been some specific gains: the quality of committee work was higher and many MPs across all parties had been persuaded of the value of the scrutiny which committees undertook "provided they didn't have to do it and it didn't detract from debates on the floor of the House!" From the Executive's perspective the assessment of the value of all-party committees was based on how far they assisted official objectives. Certainly committees dealing with race relations policy and with Scottish affairs had done much to bolster the Government's policy but most others had connected only peripherally, in Walkland's view, with main political processes.

And so, as the "coming corporatism" of Winkler's 1974 prediction seemed palpably to have arrived, and with the ignominious defeat of Mr Heath at the hands of the miners, Professor Walkland was not alone in writing so crushingly of the inadequacy of parliamentary mechanisms for influencing, let alone controlling the Government. It was, in this context not surprising that the Conservative manifesto for the 1979 election should express concern for the erosion of the role of parliament:

> The traditional role of the legislature has suffered badly from the growth of Government over the last quarter of a century. ... We will see that parliament and no other body stands at the centre of the nation's life and decisions. ... We will seek to make it effective in its job of controlling the Executive.

The sixties in retrospect

In attempting to sum up this period in the history of parliamentary reform, the following considerations are relevant. First, many of the advocates of specialist committees have presented their case by linking it to extreme assertions of parliamentary decline with the inference that this was the main solution to the problem of restoring House of Commons influence over the Executive. This case depends to some extent on whether or not the House of Commons has declined in terms of its essential function; and more importantly, on the assertion that the most important acts of the Executive, whether they are acts of policy or not, were escaping wholly from effective parliamentary control, reducing the Commons to the role of rubber stamp.

Yet the commentators who have made such a strong case for scrutiny committees on grounds of this kind have frequently watered down their proposals with reservations that would deny such committees powers to interest themselves in purely policy matters. Prior to the 1966 initiatives many advocates took care to emphasise that these committees should confine themselves to administration; see for instance the evidence of Professors Crick, Hanson and Wiseman to the Procedure Committee (HC 303, 1965).

The modesty of their proposals only serves to demonstrate that, at this stage in the process, to give specialist committees scope for intervening effectively in major policy decisions and to call the Government to account irrespective of party allegiance, would require changing the existing system of parliamentary responsibility exercised through majority parties. In fact it would require a change in the constitution which is what Professor Walkland in reviewing progress at that time, in what he termed "a liberal phase of my development", seemed to be advocating (Walkland, 1976).

In the event the very modesty of the terms of reference and activities of these committees left ministerial authority virtually impregnable to criticism. Some writers sought to preserve the distinction between policy and the administration of policy along the lines of the then Nationalised Industries Committee. Coombes (1966), for example, would have been content to see only civil servants called before committee members, leaving ministers answerable solely to the House.

In practice it is not so easy to distinguish between policy and administration and there is to some extent political policy involved in all acts of government departments quite unlike the work of nationalised industries. Moreover, if policy could be excluded from the work of select committees it is not easy to see what they could do that was different from the work of the Estimates Committee.

Both Robinson (1978) and Johnson (1966) in important studies, emphasise the centrality of public expenditure to any system of scrutiny. They single out the House of Commons Estimates Committee and its successor, the Expenditure Committee, as being illustrative of the character of parliamentary scrutiny of the administration in this period, and expose both the strengths and weaknesses of the ability of MPs to come to grips with the issues. Johnson describes the Estimates Committee as one of the most successful means of allowing MPs effective scrutiny measured simply by the sheer volume of information in its reports or by its intermittent ability to ensure that the Government was made to explain itself from time to time (Johnson, 1966, pp 12-13). Robinson, on the other hand, analysing the work of the post-1970 Expenditure Committee concludes that it had not fulfilled many of the expectations held out for it (Robinson, 1978, p 154).

These authors illustrate the divergence of view, at this stage of the debate, between those who argued for a complete new system of select committees to scrutinise and control government departments, taxation, policy and action, and those who demanded more power for the Commons in deciding the 'who gets what', of public spending in Britain (Robinson, 1978). Both stress the need for any new development of the committee system to have estimates as its focus.

The fact that these committees were not so effective, even in the limited fields to which they were assigned is one reason why they cannot be regarded as the most important cure for contemporary parliamentary and political shortcomings. The point is illustrated by Butt (1969) whose analysis of the acrimonious life and death of the Agriculture Committee and its inability to secure the information it required, demonstrates the fragile relationships which the committees of that time enjoyed with the Executive. In his view, the committee chose to examine topics of too highly a political nature and failed to maintain the support of the majority Labour Party in the House. Yet if it had voluntarily limited its activities to secondary matters it would have renounced from the start any chance of establishing a function of scrutiny or act as a corrective to failures of policy and administration. Nor did it ever gain much attention outside Westminster. The introduction, towards the end of the 1970s of a committee for Scottish affairs led Butt to suggest that this might be a more fruitful area for committee activity. Members of different parties, but representing the same area and with long experience of working together on local problems with local politicians and interest groups on the one hand and Whitehall administrators on the other, could be a useful outlet for regional discontent against the dominance of Whitehall (Butt, 1969). It was with this possibility that the debate moved forward into a wider concern for procedural reform.

The origins of reform 1976-79

The strands of the debate on the role of select committees and their piecemeal development since Crossman's 1964 innovations had by 1976 merged into a larger argument for the greater efficiency of the conduct of parliamentary business and were subsumed into a formal enquiry which was to provide the origins of the 1979 select committee system.

On 2 February 1976 the House of Commons held a whole day debate on procedure (Hansard, 1976), on a motion for the adjournment of the House, following the announcement in the Queens speech of that session, that proposals would be put forward "for a major review of the practice and procedure of parliament". A select committee on procedure was set up on the 9th June 1976 for the duration of that parliament to "consider the practice and procedure of the House in relation to public business and to make recommendations for the more effective performance of its functions" (HC 588, 1978).

In the February 1976 debate the then lord president of the council, the Right Honorable Edward Short (Lord Glenamara), suggested that at the centre of the current wave of criticism of parliament lay the relationship between the Executive and the legislature, "between the Government and parliament". In his view, the Government must govern, but be able to "secure from parliament any necessary extension of their executive powers and to implement their election pledges, by legislation or otherwise. Whatever changes we introduce should reinforce and not undermine effective Government". The tasks of parliament, on the other hand were to "set the limits of executive power and to scrutinise the exercise of executive power, to monitor our activities as a nation and to debate great issues of the day" (Hansard, 1976, col 965).

In its subsequent report which was published in July 1978 the Procedure Committee took issue with that proposition:

> We agree that the relationship between Executive and Legislature is the crucial feature of the functioning of our institutions of government, and we are conscious of the widespread concern in the country about the present nature of that relationship. But we do not believe that the criticism will be answered as Lord Glenamara's evidence suggested, merely by getting through the work demanded of the House by the Government more expeditiously and then by finding a 'worthwhile role' for the back bencher. The essence of the problem is that the balance of advantage between parliament and Government in the day-to-day working of the constitution is now weighted in favour of the Government to a degree which arouses widespread anxiety and is inimical to the proper working of our parliamentary democracy. (HC 588, 1978, p viii)

The Procedure Committee argued that a new balance must be struck, not by changes of a fundamental revolutionary character but by an evolutionary process with the prime aim of enabling the House as a whole to exercise effective control and stewardship over ministers and the expanding bureaucracy of the modern state. In addition to a wide ranging set of proposals dealing with delegated legislation, European Community (EC) legislation and Public Bill procedure, the Committee set out a detailed proposal for a new approach to select committees.

Of the system of that time, the report comments that it had developed for the most part in response to the need to relieve the pressure of business on the floor of the House or in response to new obligations or new demands for the House to perform new functions, many of which required detailed investigation unsuited to a large assembly. The system, said the report, is unplanned and unstructured:

> Surveillance of the Executive will not be substantially improved unless other reforms also take place such as the provision of more supporting staff, better financial and statistical information and more access to the floor of the House of Commons. (HC 588, 1978, p x)

Coming less than a year before the next general election it was inevitable that no action would immediately result from the Procedure Committee recommendations, but also that the debate would move from parliament to the country, and eventually to the hustings.

The Procedure Committee's deliberations had also coincided with the most intense domestic debate of the decade concerning devolution and the creation of separate assemblies for Scotland and Wales. The common theme running through all these debates was the remorseless extension of governmental activity to the extent that:

> There was now a governmental involvement in almost every aspect of an individual's life. But the existing parliamentary mechanisms were simply not enough to monitor all these multifarious activities. (Pym, 1987)

If the failure of the devolution debate prompted more attention to the possibility of special select committees for Scotland and Wales, the need for parliament to take more control of the Executive was a prime topic, especially for opposition parties in the lead-up to the 1979 general election.

In a speech to the Cambridge University Conservative Association a senior Conservative politician, referring to the Procedure Committee's report, said: "I can give a clear pledge that in the first session after a general election the next Conservative Government will present to parliament positive proposals based on this report" (Pym, 1978). At the Conservative Party Conference in that year a motion on constitutional reform, which included a reference to select committees was given a warm reception and a decision was taken by the Conservative Shadow Cabinet to include a pledge in the 1979 election manifesto.

The first Thatcher Government

Thus the rhetoric of the new Government led by Margaret Thatcher expressed a concern for the primacy of parliament and seemed determined to revamp and give teeth to another reconstruction of select committee mechanisms, this time mirroring departments rather than topics, along the lines of the Procedure Committee proposals. There was a new concern for the control of public expenditure and Norman St John Stevas, the new leader of the House, in introducing the debate on the new proposals referred to revolutionary changes:

> Today is a crucial day in the life of the House of Commons. ... We are embarking upon a series of changes that could constitute the most important parliamentary reform of the century ... intended to redress the balance of power between parliament and the Executive, to enable the House of Commons to do more effectively the job it has been elected to do. (St John Stevas, 1979)

After a full day's debate the House approved a package of reforms amounting to the establishment of a system of new 'departmental' committees. The reform left untouched many of the existing committees which dealt with the domestic running of the House and MPs' activities, those devoted to scrutiny of secondary and EC legislation and consolidation measures, and the important Public Accounts Committee (PAC).

The new structure comprised 14 committees to join the existing committees mentioned above, each shadowing a department of state, but have subsequently been increased to reflect changes in the structure of Whitehall departments. Many political actors were articulate in their advocacy of the scheme and have been, on the whole, consistent in their support since.

Edward du Cann (Conservative) and Christopher Price (Labour), both prominent back-bench committee chairs in the 1979-83 parliament, spoke enthusiastically in terms of revolutionary changes brought about by the introduction of the select committees shadowing departments of state. Du Cann predicted far reaching effects with committees undertaking a "more comprehensive and effective question time". But it is in the detailed examination of estimates and supplementary votes that he saw the potential power of select committees:

> The opportunities for the redress of small or large grievances before supply is granted will be a development the Government will be unable to resist as committees grow in stature. (Du Cann, 1981)

In a longer and more considered essay in 1984 in his role as chair of the Liaison Committee, comprising all the select committee chairs, he discounts the suggestion that the success of committees can be measured by a kind of score card of Acts which they have achieved or amended or by looking for sensational changes which they have wrung from the Government's programme (Du Cann, 1984).   Change is much more subtle: a matter of influence, of promoting change in the thinking of senior civil servants, of "unhurried-pace-setting", and of the dissemination of information to interest groups and business organisations which form the policy community around the departments concerned, to encourage the discussion of alternatives.

Price relies more upon the process and good committee management for his faith in their future.   Good leadership, bi-partisan relationships, committed staff and advisers are the best way to create genuine consensus across party lines.   As the minority party chair of the Education Science and Arts Committee (1979-83), he cites improvements in the quality of Government decision making and the injection of "an extra dimension to meetings of civil servants and ministers preparing for the announcement of new policy" (Price, 1984).

Another Labour chair John Golding experienced the process as essentially theatre, in which ministers are only too willing to appear and perform, but which has so far been avoided by the chairs of quangos and nationalised industries, a tendency which he feels must be redressed (Golding, 1984).   "Identifying the issues" was his formula for back-bench committees which, so long as every move was negotiated with his majority party vice-chair, enabled him to avoid the worst of the dissension of party-based conflict.

These and similar views were broadly echoed by many parliamentarians by the end of the 1983 session, including Biffen (1984) "a permanent feature of parliament"; Weatherill (1984) "part of our open government"; Craigen (1984) "here to stay" and Morris (1984) "a useful supplement to the armoury".

Approbation however was not universal; both in evidence to the Procedure Committee and in the debates in the House in February and June 1979 on the proposals for the new system, there was trenchant opposition to the very concept of select committees as an antidote to the power of Governments (HC 588, 1978; Hansard, 1979a; Hansard, 1979b).   In evidence to the Procedure Committee itself, Michael Foot, then lord president of the council, argued that the new committees would have the effect of transferring more and more important business away from the House of Commons chamber itself to the committee floor.   There was no substitute in his view for the open cut and thrust of party debate and the vigorous use of questions to ministers (Foot, 1976, p 63). In the subsequent debate he spoke of the need to protect "at all costs" the position of the Chamber and the rights of access of individual members - the extreme attribute of the Commons (Foot, 1979). He was echoed by Enoch Powell who argued that "everything which diminishes true debate on the floor of the House strengthens the Executive and weakens parliament" (Powell, 1979).

Willie Hamilton MP, in the debate on the substantive motion for setting up the committees contended that the whole process was "the status quo in a different wrapping. The Government are making these proposals precisely because they know they are cosmetic and will not change anything much" (Hamilton, 1979, col 99). Another MP Mr Ian Lloyd argued that the new system would involve abolishing the tried although imperfect committee system already in being and had nothing to offer for the 1980s. It would have little relevance to the technological age and would not be capable of eliciting information on computers and in other electronic storage facilities. Despite these and similar arguments, the House divided on the main question, giving approval to the proposals by 248 votes to 12.

It will be necessary to return, at the end of this work to these fears of parliamentarians and examine whether they have been justified, and whether the development of departmentally-linked scrutiny committees have indeed threatened the established practice of 'true debate' on the floor of the Commons. In the next chapter, however, the views of somewhat more detached observers of the select committees in operation in the early years of their existence will be examined.

two

THE VIEW FROM OUTSIDE

An academic assessment

If the political actors who participated in the new select committees over the first two parliaments of Margaret Thatcher were generally in support of the procedure and its potency for change, most of the academic observers point to the procedural conservatism in which the processes have been introduced and the remarkable ability of the House of Commons to maintain its institutional continuity even when, ostensibly, it is encouraging innovation. Thus Neville Johnson:

> I have never shared the optimism of the parliamentary reformers who have seen select committees as the key to changing the balance of power. ... To put the matter like this is indeed to misunderstand the problem and the prospects for the select committees. (Johnson, 1984)

If select committees have achieved a much closer relationship with government departments, Johnson believes that closer does not necessarily mean more friendly - still less collusive. He believes that the growth of specialisation amongst MPs which remains the preserve of back-bench and newer MPs, may lead in due course to changes in both the type of politician who emerges and the attitudes in the House of Commons towards its own habits and priorities. Philip Norton argues that the experience of the select committees only serves to underline the need for a far more radical reform of parliament. His approach would seek a shift in the relationship between the House of Commons and that part of it which forms the Government through an attitudinal change on the part of MPs. He does not reject structural changes and argues rather that an attitudinal change is a prerequisite to effective procedural change. It is an approach which exists independently of the Westminster model of government and does not do violence to the existing political fabric. The Norton view posits no new powers for the House of Commons and argues that the power necessary to ensure a shift in the relationships exists already: the power to defeat the Government in the division lobbies, in effect to deny legitimisation to the Government and to its measures:

> A House of Commons which exerts effective scrutiny of and influence over Government, and is seen to be performing that function, can both serve to limit the power of non-elected groups in British society and concomitantly enhance consent for the political system. (Norton, 1983)

Walkland (1985), in a rather more optimistic vein than his earlier writings, points out that MPs are really trying the impossible: to reform a system and a culture whilst at the same time remaining part of the former and being powerfully affected by the latter. "History suggests that this type of system can only be reformed through pressures external to it." But he feels the committees are serving to soften up the system from the inside even if, as Judge (1983) suggests, the participants seem so engrossed in the practice of parliamentary committee politics that they do not take time to contemplate exactly what it is that they are doing: "activity becomes a substitute for analysis" (Walkland, 1985).

Reiners (1985), in an examination of the work of the Environment Committee, suggests that given the existing disposition of powers, committees are unlikely to pose any serious threat to the Government's "elective dictatorship" and any such threat would probably ensure their demise. Their performance offers little support to the view of the Speaker, commenting on the introduction of select committees, that they would give members more power than at any time since the 17th century!

What all these contributions suggest is that the debate is constructed in terms of power and control without any attempt to define more closely the limits of those concepts, or even to ask whether it is a good thing that the legislative assembly should hold power over an elected Government.

Discussing the question of whether the 1979 reforms have turned out to be a constitutional non-event, Gavin Drewry makes the point that a constitution is partly a matter of more or less formal rules and conventions and partly a matter of attitudes and mutual understandings about "the rules of the game". It is, he concludes, a matter of what people with political influence accept as a proper way of reaching political decisions:

> Each successive stage in the development of select committees has pushed forward the base-line of MPs expectations and generated an audible click in the one way ratchet of change. Members may not as yet be clamouring for much more than they have now but would surely be unhappy to settle for less. Rising expectations may be the precondition for radical demands. (Drewry, 1985)

If indeed the process that has given rise to committee reform may be just one aspect of a pattern of growing assertiveness on the part of back-bench MPs, accompanied by greater willingness to break free of the rigid embrace of two-party adversary politics, then the hope expressed by Philip Norton that an attitudinal change effectively expressed by members can exercise the political will necessary to change the parameters within which the Government can govern may be realised.

The pressure group dimension

Richardson and Jordan (1984) have undertaken an examination of the way in which the select committee system has been used by external pressure groups. They conclude that whilst committees have been convinced by group evidence, there is doubt about the value in policy terms of winning over a select committee. Moreover they show that the kind of pressure groups selected to give evidence seem with rare exceptions to be precisely the groups who already had contacts with departments and members. They might well have been as influential in other ways. For these external organisations select committees are just one more in a range of existing means of access to the policy makers. Many retain close relations with departmental contacts, they liaise with party committees in the House and they help to develop all-party groups of MPs tending towards the formation of 'iron triangles' in the UK where groups, departments and MPs enter alliances to promote shared interests. But what about the less accepted, less 'establishment' groups with a non-specialist or an ideological point to make - or even an unpopular view to push? Is there perhaps evidence that new alliances are being formed, not with an emphasis on challenging departments or ministers but on positively promoting new policy ideas. There is not at this stage any suggestion that those on the outer reaches of pressure group activity have been brought in from the cold (Richardson and Jordan, 1984).

One example of a more tangible impact on the detail of government policy is provided in an examination by Nixon and Nixon (1983) of the work of the Social Services Committee. The committee's report on perinatal and neonatal mortality, which had been prepared in the closest cooperation with specialist and health pressure groups, found a direct response from the Department of Health and Social Security (DHSS, now DSS) which accepted a number of the committee's specific recommendations on midwifery training and has set up, under a lay chair, a Maternity Services Committee within the department. The report has helped to alert the medical and health communities generally to the problem, thus contributing to the gradual process of improving maternity and other relevant services across the country (Nixon and Nixon, 1983).

A similar positive reaction to the Social Services Committee is to be found in the department's response to a report on medical education. The main recommendation made by the committee was the need to redress the balance between consultant posts and training grade posts in the hospital service. In the Commons debate on the report, the minister of health gave a commitment to achieve the target recommended by the committee by 1988. This example seems to underline an observation by an anonymous specialist adviser to the Social Services Committee quoted by Nixon, who commented:

> The purpose of the select committee is to change the climate in which policy is made and to monitor it. This is not to assume rationality but to take rationality on board in a process which is essentially political. (Nixon and Nixon, 1983, p 353)

Party, democracy and the committee system

Jones seeks to maintain the distinction between administration and policy and finds the most satisfactory role for select committees is in concentrating on the scrutiny of the administration of the law by civil servants. He implicitly rejects the idea that back-bench MPs should have influence on policy:

> If MPs wish to engage in policy making and they are not in Government, they should operate through their party organisations. (Jones, 1984)

The response to this most basic opposition prompted Paul Griffith to return to an apparent contradiction between party government and select committee activity suggesting that it could be resolved by select committees choosing to become complementary to party government. Far from trying to seek consensus, committee members should embrace political conflict and should seek to represent conflicting perceptions within the evidence they examined. They should establish close relationships with party committees, seeking to invigorate them through the provision of relevant information (Griffith, 1985).

This is a model of party government based not on oligarchic leadership and passive interparty support but one in which initiative is dispersed to a range of forums including the parliamentary parties.

Whilst it is true that traditionally only ministers have had access to the resources of state administration, Griffiths argues that select committees could become the means to create a deconcentration of initiative within the political parties. If used for this purpose they could provide the information necessary to bridge the gap between political values and administrative experience, resource availability and opportunity cost. Brian Sedgemore had earlier recognised such a possibility too:

> The establishment of such committees would effectively disperse power in parliament and out of it into the political parties and to those groups and individuals who support political parties. (Sedgemore, 1980)

To fulfil such a role the aims and procedures of the select committees would have to change significantly. Instead of seeking an agenda that appeared to be separate from party debate and conflict, they would create an agenda based on issues actually or potentially interesting to the parties forming the House of Commons. Instead of seeking consensus they would seek information capable of contrasting interpretation and the promulgation of alternatives. Instead of seeking one agreed report they would have to produce diverse and contrasting politics. They would aim to make their impact within their own parties.

It may be thought that a considerable leap of the imagination is necessary to envisage this scenario, but Griffiths believes the result would be that parliamentary parties would come to recognise their members on select committees as indispensable assistants and researchers for party policy debate. In this way he argues the apparent contradiction between select committees and party government could be resolved. He bases his argument on an examination of one of the first reports of the newly reformed Education, Science and the Arts Committee concerning the funding of higher education, in which the committee did indeed produce two reports originating on party lines, and produced a policy outcome which Griffiths concludes allowed the minister to choose the best of both sets of arguments and justified the select committee splitting on ideological lines.

Select committees and a minority government

A new avenue of discussion is opened up with the opinion poll predictions in recent elections of a multi-party parliament or even a hung parliament in which no party has a majority. What then could be the mediating role of the select committees and could it produce a radical reconstruction of the policy making system?

If the current select committee activity is embedded firmly in the two-party system of government, would a parliament of no overall majority allow select committees to carve out an entirely new role in which they were able to harness the potential power of interest groups converting it into actual power through organisation and political action?

Such a proposition is rehearsed by Marsh (1986). He considers in some detail the possibility, hitherto largely ignored, involving the restoration of a deliberative role to the House of Commons in a hung parliament. The select committees would enjoy new powers of scrutiny and review. They would gain a place in policy making second only to that of ministers. If no party had a working majority, committees would play a vital part in building the necessary parliamentary support for Government proposals (Marsh, 1986).

Marsh accumulates evidence for the style and potential effectiveness of such a structure based upon research into the select committee activity during 1979-83. He also reviews a second role for committees, by examining their potential contribution to the integration of interest groups. He suggests there is abundant evidence of the link between interest group power and policy failure. He explores the potential to change interest group behaviour through the open and public forum provided by committees and their wider role in policy making. In what appears to be an interesting dimension to the corporatist debate, Marsh proposes the addition of an independent structure to deal with interest groups in a political context which would strengthen the mobilisation of consent in three potentially overlapping ways:

> First, policy makers could learn about interest groups views before they became publicly committed to a course of action. Second, interest groups could be presented with a variety of grounds apart from agreement for accepting proposed policies. Third, ministers would be encouraged to mobilise coalitions of interest groups to defend the course of action they proposed. (Marsh, 1986)

To accompany this process Marsh proposes that select committees should take part in a two stage budget process. The Treasury would issue a green paper or 'green budget' with preliminary departmental expenditure proposals and over a three month period leading up to the new financial year, departmental select committees would review the proposals, discuss them with affected interests and pressure groups and come forward with final proposals for departmental expenditure for agreement by the Cabinet. Committees would review the chancellor's proposals in the light of their own findings and would decide whether to recommend alternatives to the House.

The difficulty with Marsh's concept is that it would require politically committed and party activist MPs, who had fought an entirely partisan election and who would have been scrutinised by intensely political local parties, to somehow change their perspective over-night and become independent, bi-partisan animals operating largely outside a party context and without reference to party whips. This is not a scenario grounded in any sense of the reality in which political actors operate. Indeed, in a situation where a minority held the balance, party loyalty would be even more strictly enforced than where a Government held a large majority.

An administrative perspective

Very few active civil servants have commented publicly upon the impact of the new select committee system but there is a remarkable concord between those who have, summed up perhaps in the Reith lectures given by Sir Douglas Wass in 1983 in which he confirmed that the civil service was apprehensive about the new system but in the event concluded that most fears were not realised (Wass, 1984).

A number of beneficial effects have devolved to the departmental administrators he suggests: the impact on the thinking of ministers, a more rigorous approach to formulating proposals and an examination of the counter-arguments which will emerge. Wass believes that the select committees have encouraged departments to publish more information about policy and expectations and the judgements upon which they have worked and they are more likely to expose a weak ministerial case than is debated on the floor of the House. The sharpened public debate engendered by select committee reports has brought forward a wider range of interested points of view.

Wass's critical eye is not impressed, however, with the actual performance of committees and their members. He feels that witnesses on the whole are examined superficially, committee members are easily side-tracked by irrelevant evidence and comment and officials are allowed to get away with 'stone walling'. He finds a failure among committee members to prepare properly and they display poor forensic skills. The role given to specialist advisers is too dominant and they frequently end up establishing a personal point of benefit to them rather than to the committee. But the most devastating criticism he produces, and one which perhaps only a civil servant would discern, is that committees have not shown any interest in the long-term policy issues or matters which are of long-term importance. He advocates more informal and private discussion among committees and witnesses which would generate a less cautious and guarded outcome.

The first evaluations

This chapter presents two attempts by teams of academic observers to evaluate the progress of select committees after their first parliamentary term. These assessments of performance, therefore, have been limited to less than four parliamentary sessions between 1979 and 1983. They have been compiled on the basis of the output of committees, interviews with participants and commentaries by academic and political observers throughout the first Thatcher parliament.

There is a sense in which this is an inadequate basis for making judgements; most of the new committees took a long period to come to terms with their role, to reach unanimity about methodology and to get to grips with the duties placed upon them. They faced real limitations; the Government's acceptance of the Procedure Committee's general structure did not extend to some of the other recommendations, such as the provision of eight days per session for debates and more powers to enforce the attendance of ministers as witnesses and the production of papers by government departments.

Although the leader of the House had said that the Government would give "substantially increased priority" to debating select committee reports and pledged that all ministers would strive to cooperate with the new system of committees and make it a success, many advocates of the new system felt this a poor substitute for an enforceable body of procedural rules. As one close observer remarked, it is striking that "in this very serious attempt to make the investigatory committee system more effective, the new select committees were delegated no greater powers" (Lankester, 1980).

It is also clear that the pledge of cooperation from ministers did take some time to filter through to civil servants and the departmental machinery which began to feel the effect of committee enquiries (Wass, 1984).

In examining the attempts at assessment, therefore, it is necessary to acknowledge both these limitations on committee activity in the first parliament of their existence and the paucity of material with which academic observers had to work. Acceptance on the part of the Government that the committees have a role is crucial to their operation. If they have no substantive powers they have at least to have the cooperation and goodwill of the Executive and its business managers. It is the embryonic development of that goodwill as much as the immaturity of the committees' own procedures and culture which have made the first assessments of effectiveness a difficult and ultimately unsatisfactory task.

Nevertheless a team of senior academics assembled by the Study of Parliament Group monitored the committees in detail during the parliament of 1979-1983 (Drewry, 1985). There was a wide variety of styles and tone exhibited by committees: the frequency of meetings, their summons' to ministers, their style of inquisition varied greatly. The visits they made, the divisions which occurred and the length and style of their reports exhibited no uniformity at all (Lock, 1985). Lock has examined the resources, activities, visits and constitution of the committees, the attendance record of members, staffing input and costs. He concludes that there is merit in diversity and that although the 200 separate reports during the first three and a half year period included over 230 appearances by ministers and 1,800 by civil servants, 100,000 questions and 5,000 memoranda, this resulted in only 19 reports being debated in the House. Nevertheless the select committees 'had arrived'. It is, however, possible to argue that the very diversity of approach diluted the overall impact and lessened the concept of 'system' - a point which other commentators take up.

Select committees are in a sense extensions of parliament itself, designed to improve the scrutiny of the Executive, but in Drewry's terms ultimately "reflectors and reactors" striving to influence and expose but not to govern (Drewry, 1985). Whilst the inquisitorial and investigative style of committees' activities has advantages over the adversarial clashes on the floor of the House, it is itself subject to criticism, suggests Drewry, that the selection of topics is too much influenced by the need to avoid the party political issues and that the lack of expert inquisitors prevents sharply focused interrogation. The debate as to how best to ensure that select committees specialise and whether it should be by department, by topic or subject area, has gone on for at least 70 years (Haldane, 1918) and is now somewhat overtaken by the fact that the new committees can, in any case, select virtually any subject they like and have given themselves "considerable latitude" in dealing with issues which may fall into more than one departmental remit (HC 588, 1978).

Indeed later chapters will demonstrate the point quite clearly: one benefit arising from the Trade and Industry Committee study of waste reclamation was to highlight the conflict of approach within different ministries, and to show that no ministry had a policy to deal with waste reclamation. Similarly, the Committee for Welsh Affairs study of coastal pollution demonstrates the need for a corporate strategy by the Department of the Environment (DOE), Ministry of Agriculture, Fisheries and Food (MAFF), Welsh Office and the public bodies which they sponsor.

Thus the flexibility which committees assume in choosing topics is not only a benefit, it has proved vitally important in exposing the lack of coordination or corporate approach in government.

A more substantive criticism of the new select committees is the lack of any systematic approach (Drewry, 1985). Whilst the establishment of a Liaison Committee of chairs of select committees and the informal network of clerks and officials may prevent overlapping, the very looseness of the terms of reference and the diverse approach of members themselves militate against a rigid systematic approach to departmental scrutiny. Is this a bad thing? An experienced committee chair's view is that part of the skill in exerting maximum influence is to choose topics which either are or are about to surface as matters of public concern, and to 'get in early' with a searching factual review which can be respected, non-partisan, well researched and constructive in its recommendations (Rossi, 1987). In this sense, ad hoc selection of topics is not just beneficial, but a positive skill.

Observers of committees during the 1979-83 parliament noted a consistent reluctance to fulfil that part of the terms of reference dealing with departmental expenditure. Robinson (1985) took a special interest in this area, and concluded that members have collectively made clear that they are not prepared to undertake regular and thorough scrutiny of main estimates each year as a matter of routine, and indeed have not shown much enthusiasm for financial duties. Most financial recommendations arise as a result of, or a by-product of, 'policy' enquiries. Indeed Robinson categorises select committees as being either "spending committees", processing demands for more public expenditure, or "balancing committees", which attempt to weigh the demands for extra spending against value for money orders and cost control. A third group make no clear judgements either way on the financial implications of their recommendations.

Drewry's (1985) analysis leads him to the conclusion that the best recipe for success is the coming together of a group of knowledgeable members with an informal interest in a subject, working constructively together; in these circumstances, he suggests, it does not matter whether the topic is potentially politically explosive, or a relatively 'safe' one. However, he does not quite answer his own question: "what constitutes success?" Are the 1979 reforms simply 'new labels on old bottles'? Drewry's team come to the broad conclusion that they are not, but admit that to demonstrate the proposition is not easy.

Giddings (1985) takes the argument on, detecting the beginnings of a willingness of some members in the context of monolithic party domination, to unite across parties in a spirit of 'control of the Executive', with a growing number of MPs seeing their role as much in these terms as in supporting their own front benches. In terms of impact upon policy making, Giddings reads the input of select committees rather less positively; it is "just one more factor which whips, ministers and administrators have to take into account; just part of the input into the continuing process of government". He concludes that committee reports can generate publicity, provide a platform for interest groups, and gather information, but they cannot be measured simply in terms of recommendations which are accepted; rather by the long-term effects of keeping decision makers on their toes and making them justify themselves. In this, their influence has been indirect, marginal, contextual rather than substantive.

The impact of committees in the wider public arena in their first parliament was less than dramatic. Giddings' conclusion (1985, p 380) is that interest in their activities had not spread much beyond established communities of interest; he detects no significant widening of these policy communities, no basic change in the pattern of relationships in the British parliamentary system.

Very much the same range of conclusions is arrived at in an important symposium and workshop organised in 1983 by the research subcommittee of the Public Administration Committee of the Joint University Council for Social and Public Administration, subsequently published by Strathclyde University (Hill, 1984). A mix of academic observers and key political actors examine the first three and a half years of select committee performance. This symposium discerns two major features of select committee activity in the early years. First, the committees' activities help to put topics on the political agenda and submit ministers to a level of questioning not available in the House, and provide a threat of scrutiny to a wide range of a department's affairs. Second, and in contrast, the committees remain 14 separate and different bodies which do not constitute a system. The activities of committees are not linked in any formal way to the work of the House but nevertheless do complement the House in a way which earlier committees had not done. Hill (1984) describes committee members more as shrewd political laypeople rather than experts who appear to welcome the opportunity which committee work provides, both for informing themselves and for criticising departments. This may also be an outlet for MPs' frustration with the inadequacies of Commons procedures and, without proposing a conspiracy theory, she poses the question: "are they just devices to keep members happy?" Her conclusion was 'no', the House is an evolutionary chamber and committees are a successful development albeit unsystematic, small and with minuscule staff support by international standards (Hill, 1984).

The symposium concludes that the success of the new committees is in informing and scrutinising activities which were always a part of parliament's functions. They have enhanced this role, not altered it dramatically (or constitutionally) and in so doing they have strengthened the dialogue among members of the policy community broadly conceived: MPs, ministers, civil servants, departments, interest groups, academics and the informed media. Again, committees can (though as yet they have not got the balance exactly right) develop current topics and longer-term enquiries. Evaluating success in terms of recommendations accepted or policy altered is marginal. Hill sums up this wide ranging examination with the comment:

> Committees have been a success in altering the perceptions and behaviour of Whitehall. Though they are by no means a fierce threat to departments, the evidence suggests that no big new policy will be made without ministers and mandarins anticipating very carefully the information that committees will seek. People are more aware that their decisions may be questioned and while this may not mean that the decision is changed it ensures that the surroundings to that decision are fully explored. It is a desirable outcome that civil servants themselves have had to expound on policies to committee members and have had to be capable of explaining the reasons behind those policies. The principle remains intact that in so doing civil servants are accountable to ministers and not to the committees themselves. The conclusion must be that the policy process has changed; whether policy itself has changed will have to await further study. (Hill, 1984)

However, since this review was undertaken a number of incidents have occurred which have heightened the tension between the Government and committees and led some commentators to suggest that there are signs that their powers are being resisted. The resignation of Michael Heseltine as secretary of state for defence following the Cabinet argument over the future of

Westland Helicopters subsequently surfaced in examinations of the Government's conduct by three separate select committees - Trade and Industry, Treasury and Civil Service, and Defence. It is clear that Heseltine had utilised the Defence Select Committee in support of his ongoing strategy for the Westland company and had orchestrated back-bench and press support in a series of contacts with committee members, both by himself and his departmental officials. The constitutional argument which followed resulted in a crucial House of Commons debate on the 15th January 1985 on the Opposition's motion calling upon the Government to "make arrangements to set up a committee of the House" to consider the Westland affair. In the event this was rejected in favour of a Government amendment recognising the competence of departmental select committees to consider issues raised by these developments. There is, then, an element of paradox in a situation where a beleaguered Government actually welcomes the critical scrutiny of select committees and which leads Drewry to detect both a hint of contempt for the perceived marginality of the departmental committees and a whiff of fear at the likely outcome of the alternative (Drewry, 1987). The Government was subsequently unwilling to give the committee all the cooperation that it requested.

Similarly the Bank of England refused to supply a list of documents relating to the Tin crisis of 1986 to the Trade and Industry Select Committee and the prime minister made clear her opposition to the degree to which civil servants were obliged to answer questions about their conduct in some circumstances. Thus Anthony Beaumont-Dark, a Conservative back bencher: "Governments want parliament to be a dog that wags its tail - they don't mind every now and then parliament barking but they don't like it to bite".

three

THE CONCEPT OF SYSTEM

The need for systematic measurement

All of this closely observed analysis remains subjective, partial and lacking in any form of measurement or quantification; nor does it propose any theoretical basis relating the operational methods of committees to their ability to influence policy. The observers of select committees' first parliament broadly agree on the limited range of their influence but it remains insubstantial - slipping like jelly through the fingers before it can be evaluated. What influence, how much and in what conditions? If some are more influential than others, why and in what circumstances?

On the basis of three full parliaments of committee functioning is it still the case, as Giddings (1985) suggests, that their impact on ministerial and departmental policy has been indirect, marginal, and contextual rather than substantive? Or that they are cosy, non-partisan cliques remote from the real world of confrontational politics? Such critics can only be refuted by the production of convincing evidence of the positive achievements of committees and by demonstrating their effectiveness in furthering the ends of the House of Commons.

This study proposes an analysis which utilises a systematic evaluation of the inputs and outputs of the select committee process and relates them to the type of issue being examined, and to the 'mode' or tone and approach of the committee in its conduct of the investigation and its examination of witnesses and evidence. A matrix is proposed in which these elements of the process are related to one another and to the fate of the committees' formal recommendations. A further dimension of the evaluation is provided in the proposition that the degree of influence achieved may depend upon the point in the policy process at which a particular report attempts to intervene. This requires an examination of the range and nature of influences which select committees have at their command and will require a far wider concept than the one which suggests that 'influence' is limited to the degree to which the Executive is persuaded to modify policy or introduce new policy. The proposition will need to rely on a model of the policy process in a parliamentary democracy and to theorise select committee activity in terms of a modified miniature version of the larger political system.

The hypothesis proposed here is, first, that the establishment of a measurable formula of select committee activity will enable a more measured view to be taken of their influence and, by reference to reports published in the field of environmental policy during the parliament of 1983-87, allows a post hoc testing of the methodology. Second, that the degree of influence thus achieved may also be dependent upon the point in the policy process at which 'intervention' is attempted. The closely observed academic and participative analysis of earlier accounts by key actors and political scientists referred to in the preceeding chapters may, therefore, be supplemented by a more systematic approach, relying somewhat on the factual analysis of inputs, outputs, outcomes and issue types.

It is argued here that what select committees have done is to create sub-systems, mirroring the political system, using the same policy communities, and utilising the same kinds of input, stimuli and processes. But instead of 'policy' emerging as the output from the machine, we have, in effect, challenges to policy, intervention, scrutiny or questioning, all of which have the potential to become a modification of, or addition to, the very policy they have been examining. In order to demonstrate this hypothesis, concepts of political activity as system and a sound notion of policy as process need to be established or adapted.

Parliament as system

Giddings's (1985) reference above to the "continuing process of government", suggests the need to establish the place of select committees in the political system, and the theorisation of select committee activity within that system. Even acknowledging Hill's reservation on this point, (see p 34) the concept of politics as a system for the analysis of policy development has increasingly been established in academic writing since the 1960s. Writers such as Easton (1965), Ham and Hill (1984), and Hogwood and Gunn (1984) all use the concept for analysing decision making as a method of converting inputs into outputs in the form of policies, laws, procedures, goods or services.

In a generalised form this model points up the relationship between demands, the political system, the outputs of the system and the impact of these outputs in terms of stabilising the environment or setting off new demands via a feedback process (see Figure 1). This figure also emphasises the cyclical nature of much policy activity.

As Hogwood (1987) has noted, however, as an aid to understanding the functions of the state and how policy gets made, it suffers from being very general and unspecific and as such contains serious defects. First, this framework says nothing about how inputs are transformed into outputs; it treats the decision making process as a 'black box'. It tells us nothing about the distribution of power or the substance of policies. Second, the model operates at too high a level of generality and has been likened by Burch and Wood (1983) to a sausage factory production process.

Nevertheless it does at least establish that the political system maintains its existence by responding to the changes in the environment although it has little to say about which changes matter politically and why particular policies are evolved in response to them. Third, the simplified systems model might imply that decision making only occurs on and reflects demand articulation. In practice political demands may be shaped or even created by political leaders, as Ham and Hill (1984) have demonstrated.

Figure 1: Easton's model of the political system

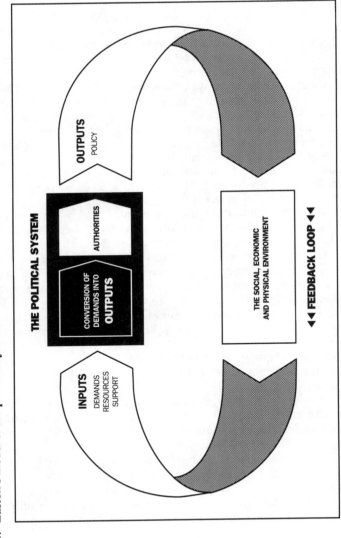

Source: Derived from Easton (1965)

Committee activity as system

In this study, however, the model is adapted to describe the processes at work in the activities of select committees which themselves can be described and explained in terms of the inputs they receive and the outputs they produce. In that context, and in the singular conditions of a specific committee enquiry, the activity does indeed operate as a systematic series of activities. These commence as stimulation from the environment and lead to inputs, negotiated or assessed outputs; possible outcomes which may in turn produce renewed or cyclical repercussions. One way of refining the concept and to meet the 'sausage machine' criticism is to develop it in more detail and adapt it in terms of the organisations involved in the process, to move away from generality and apply to the model the numerous participants in the activities of input and output.

Whilst select committees are not primary policy makers, and have to operate at the boundaries between the Executive and the Legislature, in balance between whips and back-bench and between party faction, there is an inevitability of mutual adjustment, pluralism, consensus-seeking and incrementalism. Their activities are nevertheless grounded in the day-to-day minutiae of policy and decision making. The processes of policy monitoring and the examination of expenditure, administration and policy, call for approaches which can equally be explained in terms of inputs and outputs.

Thus, by adapting the Easton (1965) model of the political system, the activities of select committees can be illustrated as in Figure 2.

The model illustrated in Figure 2 indicates the process of select committee investigations and their function of forming a bridge between parliamentary activity and the interests represented outside that system. The origins of topics which may eventually emerge as a subject for investigation can be various. Once the investigation is underway, inputs to the system range from memoranda and oral evidence to a wide range of witnesses and specialist advisers and experts, to the detailed briefings provided by committee officers and the visits of the committee members themselves.

Figure 2: A model of select committee activity devised from Easton's 'black box' model of the political system

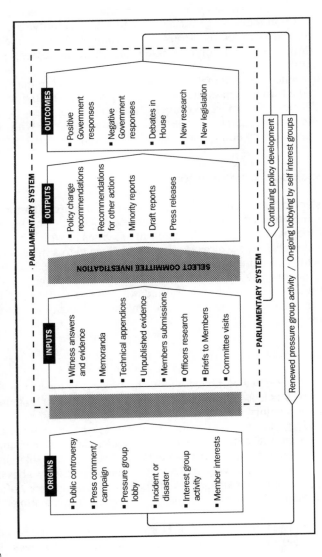

Source: Derived from Easton (1965)

The output of this system model might come in the form of recommendations, minority reports, press releases and the committees' substantive reports to parliament. These may then lead to a range of outcomes which may be positive or negative. Responses by the Government to committee recommendations come initially in the form of further parliamentary activity, such as debates on the floor of the House, Government or departmental action, further research of the issue or, in some cases, new legislation.

Further outcomes external to the parliamentary system may also follow in the form of renewed pressure group activity, lobbying and public debate. Or, more positively, there are examples of the continuing development of the policy under review with the department or policy community actively involved.

The 'black box' phenomenon

The system model falls short of a comprehensive explanation of select committee activity in two important respects. The shaded areas of the diagram (Figure 2) represent activities in which it is not clear what processes are at work. It may be likened to a mechanical device which contains at key points, sealed boxes with the legend: 'only to be opened by an officially approved mechanic'. The activity within remains a mystery and we need to understand the influences and functions at work in both locations of the mechanism.

The first sealed box

The first of these sealed boxes within the process is located at the point where a select committee, faced with a number of potential subjects for enquiry in the form of public controversy, pressure group activity or some stimulus external to the parliamentary system, have to make choices as to which topics they will consider. The process is a complex and delicate one: sifting and selecting. The box is 'sealed' in a very real sense in that the activity goes on either in private informal sessions of the committee or, more often in the domain of officers and advisers outside the meetings of members.

The activity is, in the terms of Hogwood's (1987) analysis, (see Figure 3, p 54) one of issue search or agenda setting, followed by issue filtration; of deciding to decide and deciding how to decide. This involves the identification of problems or of opportunities for committee enquiry, of sifting from possible topics those which, once chosen, form the agenda for the committee and the policy community which will be involved in the enquiry.

As described by key participants in the Environment Committee, a list of possible topics will be drawn up by the clerk to the committee. He or she will have in mind the chair's own stated view of the kind of issues appropriate for select committee investigation (HC 363, 1984/5) and will add to the list any items which the chair specifically proposes (Gren, 1987). The list is submitted to an informal meeting of the committee when other possible topics may be raised by members. The discussion will include an assessment of how much impact could be achieved, how much press coverage and public interest would be generated and whether the subject was relevant in a policy context to current public policy issues.

It is clear from the evidence that the dominant input to the decision will be that of the chair and his or her committee officer, especially in circumstances where at the beginning of a new parliament they are the only two participants with a continuity from the previously constituted committee, most other MPs being newly appointed. This point is illustrated in the constitution of the Environment Committee at the beginning of the 1987 Parliament, compared with its changing membership between 1983 and 1987, as shown in Table 1.

Seven out of the original eleven members served throughout the 1983-87 parliament. Of the remainder two served for more than two years and two for periods of from seven months to sixteen months. Of the replacement members only one stayed for two years, the remainder for a few months. However, when the committee reformed after the election of 1987 only five of its members came from the previous parliament, one of whom was Sir Hugh Rossi, again appointed chair. Of the other six none had served the previous committee throughout its existence.

The activities of pressure groups and media coverage of topics such as green belt policy or acid rain pollution will have influenced the collation of the original list of topics and it is likely that any topic with a currently high profile, "but not in a party political context", will be considered (Gren, 1987). Once a topic or policy issue is identified there will be a further discussion among members about the possibility of witnesses and specialist advisers, visits to be made and a degree of conflicting interest group response which will be generated. The process of "deciding to decide", then, is likely to be led strongly by officer and chair but, "only so long as the members retain trust in them and after that trust has been earned" (Gren, 1987).

Table 1:   Membership of the Environment Select Committee 1983-87 and 1987-92

		1983-87 Parliament (Appointed December 1983)		1987-92 Parliament (Appointed November 1987)
Name	Party	Appointed	Discharged	
Rossi, Sir Hugh	C	Dec. 1983	dissolution	reappointed
Alexander, R.	C	Dec. 1983	dissolution	
Alton, D.	Lib	Dec. 1983	Apr. 1986	
Eyre, Sir R.	C	Dec. 1983	July 1984	
Chapman, S.	C	Dec. 1983	dissolution	
Critchley, J.	C	July 1984	Apr. 1985	
Freeson, R.	L	Dec. 1983	Apr. 1985	
Jones, R.B.J.	C	Dec. 1983	Nov. 1986	reappointed
Miscampbell, N.	C	Dec. 1983	dissolution	
Roberts, A.	L	Dec. 1983	dissolution	
Smith, C.	L	Dec. 1983	dissolution	
Taylor, J.M.	C	Dec. 1983	dissolution	
Mckay, A.	C	Apr. 1985	Feb. 1986	
Pike, P.	L	Apr. 1985	dissolution	reappointed
Holt, R.	C	Feb. 1986	dissolution	reappointed
Stern, M.	C	June 1986	June 1987	
Hunter, A.	C	Nov. 1986	dissolution	reappointed
Sayeed, J.	C	Jan. 1987	dissolution	
Bellingham, H.	C	Nov.1987		
Boateng, P.	L	Nov.1987		
Cummings, J.	L	Nov.1987		
Mans, K.	C	Nov.1987		
Pendry, T.	L	Nov.1987		
Squire, R.	C	Nov.1987		

The second sealed box

The work of the committee in formal session, or on visits, is more complex than published proceedings would imply. It is in this activity of the actual select committee investigation, and the way in which all the inputs suggested in Figure 2 are digested and emerge as output, that the second 'sealed box' is sited and needs further clarification.

All potential witnesses are first asked to submit written memoranda (Gren, 1987). A selection of potential oral witnesses is then prepared by officers with assistance from specialist advisers and is submitted to the chair and then to the committee for approval. Officers also prepare synopses of written evidence submitted, together with detailed briefings on the issue involved. An important role for the specialist adviser will be to prepare a list of suggested questions which members will ask witnesses, in order that key parts of their evidence are properly exposed (Gren, 1987).

It would seem from this descriptive evidence by key actors in the Environment Committee that most members of the committee play a passive role in the proceedings. A strong chair with a clearly articulated view of the committee's role, allied to an able committee clerk provide most of the impetus and direction. Busy MPs are, it would appear, willing to submit to a somewhat directive process, provided that the officials have regard to the political sensitivities and are competent and thorough in their administration, and also that the chair's formula as exposed above, delivers positive responses, a favourable public and press reaction and a degree of respect from within the policy community related to the particular topic under investigation. The sifting of evidence and the drafting of the committee's report and recommendations follow a similarly collaborative procedure; the committee clerk providing initial drafts for the chair and with his or her amendments, for subsequent private sessions of the committee. Members will, in informal session, negotiate amendments and frame detailed recommendations; only in formal sessions of the committee are amendments officially tabled and voted upon - an unusual circumstance in the context of the Environment Committee.

Theoretical perspectives

But this descriptive account of the activities which take place is not, in itself, sufficient to understand what is going on. For a deeper understanding of the way in which committee outputs are produced it is necessary to look at theoretical concepts; to focus attention upon the nature of interactions in these 'sealed boxes', involving consideration of the power-interest structures and relationships between participating actors and agencies. This may lead to a clearer understanding of the way 'policy' - or in this case, committee recommendations - are mediated, negotiated and modified, and then brought to legitimation in the final report.

For Bacharach and Lawler (1980) this emphasis on groups and interaction is central; organisations are viewed as aggregates of groups constituting bargaining systems. The main activity is in mobilising interests or forming coalitions aimed at influencing authoritative decisions or recommendations.

Alliances between agents within the system and those outside are a particularly interesting area of activity arising from the new select committee system. Those within the system seeking change or opposing vested interests reach for alliances which will assist their case or supply additional arguments or information. Those whom Deakin (1986) has termed "policy entrepreneurs" will cultivate appropriate contacts in the wider policy community, just as outsiders seeking change cultivate parliamentary contacts. Select committees represent a so far underdeveloped resource in the complex undertaking of seeking change in a pluralist democracy.

In our context, however, coalitions are not part of the formal structure but emergent products of the informal processes that are essential to organisational politics. In the committee process described above, the potential for coalitions is evident. The dominance of the collaboration between the chair and the committee clerk has been described; in addition the party caucuses of members, relationships between individual members and pressure groups or external interests, are all potential power alliances. There is evidence too, from the recorded proceedings and the comments of participants, of a kind of professional corporatism among the scientific and specialist advisers and witnesses acting for various groups. In complex topics expertise is itself a form of power.

Who has power in the process is another crucial element in the bargaining process. The formal power of the chair and the members with votes is mitigated by that of the officer corps who negotiate evidence, brief the witnesses and plan the proceedings, and actually write draft reports and recommendations. There is power too in specialist knowledge particularly in highly scientific subjects and by the relationships forged within the policy community providing inputs to the committee investigation. For example, in the investigation of major planning enquiries, the chairs of the nationalised industries collectively made the case for less planning constraints on their activities in a powerful joint paper (HC 181 1986, vol II, p 63).

Pfeffer's (1981) concern with power relationships is relevant here. In his work on organisational politics he stresses that power is a function of both the actors' positions in the social structure and their "net dependancy relationships". But the accounts of committee activity described above seem to demonstrate that power is not something formally distributed or embodied in the structure of the system but rather characterises relationships between individuals and groups. In other words, it is characteristic of the pattern of interaction within the select committee and in the contacts it has with the witnesses, the experts, the civil servants and pressure groups who make supplication to it.

By focussing on bargaining among political actors we may neglect to theorise the administrative activity, the role of the clerk and the machine which links him or her to departmental civil servants and Whitehall. If earlier comments stress the theoretical tenets of organisational politics and decision making within select committees, there is also a need to synthesise them with a theory more related to bureaucratic politics. It should be clear that select committee work is almost wholly conducted in a bureaucratic context and the evidence above suggests a significant role for key functionaries. It is administered within the parliamentary administrative machine, its own bureaucracy interacting with that of Whitehall at all times.

Jenkins and Gray (1983) emphasise the need to study bureaucracies as political organisations, and here the literature on organisational power and politics is helpful for, as Pfeffer (1981) notes, the issue is less about free action versus structurally determined behaviour as about influencing choice under constraint: about factors such as task, resource control and structure.

What this adds up to is that to detect what goes on in the sealed boxes of the select committee system it should be recognised that the power networks and coalitions described in theories of organisational politics are modified in this context by the bureaucratic political behaviour of the committee administrators. Specifically they appear to have direct influence at three levels of behaviour. First, they influence the way some issues get on the agenda and others do not. Second, they constrain the perception and appreciation of issues and interests: that is they have important influence over witnesses, specialist advisers and the flow of information as well as the legal and regulatory procedures of the House of Commons. Third, they may shape the resulting actions, recommendations and responses. Whilst not wishing to offer this as a comprehensive explanation, it is suggested that it does explicitly recognise the dynamics of bureaucratic politics in public administration and that political conflict and bargaining can be only a partial explanation of decision making.

If this is an accurate account of what happens in the sealed boxes of the 'mini-system' of the select committee, we need to turn now to the means open to committees to fulfil their ambition of influencing what happens in that larger and more significant 'black box' in the middle of the parliamentary political system (see Figure 1) to make sense of the multitude of ways that political activity emerges as 'policy'.

If the writers reviewed earlier are right that committee influence has been indirect, marginal and lacking in substance they have certainly not made much progress in opening up the black box or modifying its processes.

The next chapter seeks to understand these mechanisms in a way which would illustrate the most effective modes of committee intervention and to discover what Jenkins and Gray (1983) call the "focal points of bargaining and conflict".

four

INTERVENTION: THE CRITICAL ISSUE

The point of impact

It is the contention of this chapter that one of the factors governing the degree of success of select committees in influencing the policy and practice of Governments, is the point at which their reports and recommendations impact upon the activities of Government decision making. This notion is akin to the view of a leading committee chair expressed earlier, that there is some skill involved in choosing investigation topics which will loom large in the public interest and in the media, without necessarily being of acute party political controversy (Rossi, 1987).

The point is given support by the suggestion in Jenkins and Gray (1983, p 181) that organisations can be viewed as aggregates of groups constituting bargaining systems: "the making of decisions in the organisation is the focal point for bargaining and conflict". They cite Bacharach and Lawler's (1980) claim that organisational politics involves the mobilising of interest groups aimed at influencing authoritative decisions; a very apposite description of a select committee at work.

The examination of a series of reports on environmental topics (see Chapters 6 to 8) will analyse not only the kind of issue and mode of investigation which the committee adopted but will propose that, dependant upon the topic under review and the way in which the recommendations are framed, the committee report will have the effect of intervening at a particular point in the wider policy machinery of the parliamentary system. For example, the committee may propose an entirely new policy and attempt to get a subject into the Government's legislative programme. It might stimulate a review or new evaluation of long-standing policy content, or, particularly in examining complex technical subjects, provide advice and information to a department in the work of forecasting; that is to say making and evaluating assumptions about the future context of contemporary decisions. Yet again, the way in which a committee deals with expert witnesses and sifts contrasting technical evidence may be an important contribution to the analysis of options which confront the primary policy makers within the executive machine.

Thus we must examine the possibility that committees may be more successful in influencing policy if their reports attempt to intervene at some points in the policy process rather than at others.

Models of the policy process

A necessary prior step in pursuing this proposition is to seek an appropriate model of policy making; to examine a variety of approaches to the theorisation of the way public policy gets made, and to select one which could facilitate the testing of the hypothesis described above.

In the context of this book it is helpful to relate the concept of political activity taking place within a system, to the description of policy making as process, and to envisage both notions as taking place within a social and economic environment rather than simply as the detached activity of remote executive decision makers.

Academic interest in policy analysis in the last 40 years has been concerned with both prescriptive and descriptive propositions: how does it happen and how should it happen? Writers in the tradition of Simon (1958) have proposed ideal type models, relying upon rational means of isolating objectives and selecting the most appropriate means to secure ends. In later work, Simon and others have proposed to "satisfice"; to accept that what is theoretically ideal may not be possible in practice for lack of information or resources, and therefore to accept that the central concern of administrative theory should be with the boundary between the rational and the non-rational or realistic aspects of human and social behaviour - with "bounded rationality".

Simon (1958, p 241) suggests that policy makers are also limited by the values, conceptions of purpose, habits and reflexes of the individual who can respond in rational terms to the organisation's goals only to the extent that he or she is able, informed and can comprehend. Only within the bounds laid down by these factors are his or her choices rational and goal-oriented.

In this sense, as Hogwood and Gunn suggest (1984, p 44) rationality models are posing the question: "how would policies be made if we were all capable of perfect rationality?" Contrasting with these notions, adherents of other descriptive models apply what Allison (1971) has called "a conceptual lens" through which we view our activity and try to make sense of it. Writers such as Lindblom (1959) dilute the importance of rationality in favour of the concept of "successive limited comparisons". Whilst the rational-comprehensive approach is the base or starting point, he suggests that real policy development starts from an existing situation and changes by small incremental steps. The test of success is not whether the policy maximises the values of the decision maker but whether it secures the agreement of the interests involved. He argues that incrementalism, or "muddling through", is both a good description of how policy is actually made and a model for how it should be done. To muddle through more effectively is better than to aim for some super-human comprehensiveness (Lindblom, 1959, p 88).

The difficulty for the would-be analyst of the role of select committees in the policy arena is that by applying Allison's (1971) "conceptual lens" to the day-to-day life of the members and officers of state and parliamentary institutions it is only too clear that in the vast array of institutions which make up the state, there are cross-cutting elements of each of these concepts bound up in their activities. Indeed, for those theorists who have looked to find concepts of power and decision making in examining theories of the role of the state, there are strands in the political system which echo all major theoretical constructs in modern writing. Ideas of elite theory, of bureaucratic power, of corporatist relationships, or pluralistic policy making can all be detected both in the mega-system and in committee activity. Marxists too would find support for their theories in the links between some committees - notably the Trade and Industry Committee and the Energy Committee - and the economic interests of capitalist industries, and would point to these interests as a means of maintaining the dominance of particular social classes, just as much as in their concept of the state itself.

For the purposes of this chapter, however, we are less concerned with grand theory than with finding a satisfactory way of describing the step-by-step progression of issue into proposal and into policy. With that tool to hand it will be possible to test the idea that the influence of select committees may vary dependant upon the point in that process at which they intervene.

What is of interest then is the emergence of policy and the concept of step-by-step process, with an understanding of the interactions among a widespread range of participants: self-interest groups, pressure groups, professionals and civil servants. The ideas of Hogwood and Gunn (1984) fulfil this need. They also have in common with many of the writers mentioned above, the concept of cycle, complementing the political system model.

Hogwood and Gunn propose a mixed framework for the analysis of policy which has as its defining characteristic a prescriptive aspect; a bias towards the improvement of policy processes. It is 'mixed' in a number of senses. First, it can be used for both prescription and description, and second, it does not conform rigidly to either the rational or to the incremental notions discussed above. It provides, not so much a middle way as a recognition that the appropriate mode of analysis will depend upon the issue and the context. Finally, it is mixed in that it is concerned both with the application of techniques for analysis and also political process.

The process is envisaged in nine stages thus:

(i)   deciding to decide (issue search or agenda-setting);

(ii)   deciding how to decide (or issue filtration);

(iii)   issue definition;

(iv)   forecasting;

(v)   setting objectives or priorities;

(vi)   options analysis;

(vii)   policy implementation, monitoring and control;

(viii)   evaluation and review;

(ix)   policy maintenance, succession or termination.

These are the stages through which an issue may pass although the authors stress that this will not happen in every case; rather it is a framework for organising an understanding of what may happen or not happen. The process may be truncated, or in some cases be reordered, and the dividing lines between one point and another may be blurred.

The difficulty for analysts is to bring some semblance of order to the disaggregated manner in which policy is initiated, processed and shaped in the complex environment of British government, and indeed to ask whether or not any idea of coordinated or rational policy making may be a myth. Hogwood (1987), in a later work, builds on the theoretical framework discussed here and sets out to chart the emergence of policy in practice, allowing issues to surface and become shaped by institutions, groups and key actors. He suggests there is no one way of characterising or defining public policy, but for the purposes of this book, by utilising his cyclical concept the influences which are at work may be more readily understandable, and it can be seen how the activities of select committees impinge upon them.

Particular attention is paid here to implementation and the difficulty of linking outputs to intentions. Specifically, to the developing capacity of committees to undertake evaluation and to a discussion as to whether the select committee system may be moving British government from what Jenkins (1988) has called "its usual state of complacency".

In attempting to utilise this approach in the context of select committee intervention, it is necessary to avoid a too slavish devotion to the well-organised yet essentially idealistic and atheoretical model and to make two modifications to the Hogwood and Gunn (1984) concept. First, a tenth stage must be added to the list: that of 'feedback' to recognise the fact that the outcome of policy often does cause repercussions or a renewal of the cycle of activity. Second, and in order to illustrate more readily the proposal that select committees may intervene at any point, to illustrate the concept in circular form (see Figure 3, p 54). This gives added point to the cyclical or continuing nature of the process and complements the models of both parliamentary and committee activity illustrated above.

Having thus established a theoretical pattern of policy making in action, which describes what is actually going on at any stage, we can now examine the proposition that some of the stages in the process may be more susceptible to intervention by a select committee enquiry than others.

Figure 3:   A model of the policy process adapted from Hogwood and Gunn

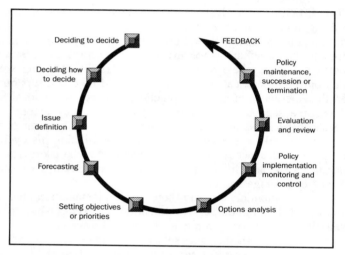

Source: Derived from Hogwood and Gunn (1984)

A well-researched report, on a topic of current public interest, which achieves debate on the floor of the House and argues authoritatively for change, may have much impact at the time the department is seeking definitions or choosing options; would it have the same impact if the department was deep into the implementation programme?

These questions may be answered more surely if there is an examination of the type of issue under discussion and the approach which the committee takes; ie the mode it adopts within the 'second sealed box' referred to in Figure 2 above. The concept of 'mode' and the relevance of the issue type are examined in more detail in the next chapter.

five

STYLE AND CONTENT AS FACTORS OF SUCCESS

Committee mode

This chapter argues that 'success' for a select committee measured by the degree of influence it is able to exert on policy or departmental practice, will depend upon a number of factors. The type of issue being investigated will be important, and as has been argued in the previous chapter, so will the point in the policy cycle at which intervention is attempted. But another factor which may have a bearing concerns the particular approach, style or method which the investigation adopts. The stance taken initially on the issue, the approach to witnesses and indeed the kind of arguments which are deployed, all go to make up the mode of an enquiry.

Indeed, committees may have differing purposes for differing reports. It may be that they aim to influence a department or another public sector agency, or to inform members for a forthcoming debate, or again to provide a platform for external interests. These variations in goals or purposes are an important ingredient in determining mode.

It will be seen that the mode may vary from committee to committee and, within a committee, from enquiry to enquiry and will be influenced by the way the issue was raised at the outset. In the course of examining ten major committee investigations on environmental topics produced in the 1983-87 parliament, a number of modes adopted by committees can be detected. They fall into distinctly separate types.

At times select committees appear to take an approach which is essentially that of advocating new policy, attempting to get new matter on to the political agenda and proposing policy innovation. In other instances the dominant mode is one of analysing existing policy failure, reviewing departmental performance or policy effectiveness.

In some investigations it is possible to characterise the role of select committees as providing a platform for conflicting interest groups: mediating between, for example, environmental pressure groups and industrial producer organisations or self-interest groups; seeking an acceptable formula for policy advance and prioritising conflicting interests and issues.

Finally, there is a mode or approach to investigations which is overtly aggressive and confrontational and in which the committees essentially challenge ministers to explain, and expose poor performance or implementation.   See Figure 4 below for a summary of these modes.

Figure 4:   Dominant themes in the concept of 'mode'

Mode	Dominant themes
Advocating/ agenda-setting	Policy innovation; channelling public opinion to Government; tabling new issues.
Analysis and review	Analysis of existing policies and performance; tabling new arguments or recent thinking; scrutiny of administrative efficiency; examination of appropriateness and effectiveness of policy objectives; exposing conflicting policy aims and inter-departmental contradictions; forecasting outcomes.
Mediation and prioritising	Providing platform for conflicting interests; suggesting compromise solutions; prioritising policy objectives; resolving conflicts within policy community; clarifying aims of legislation and mediating disparate interests.
Challenging and monitoring	Seeking explicit ministerial objectives or Government intention; exposing policy failure; exposing policy 'vacuum'; objectives analysis; monitoring the development of policy.

The hypothesis explored here is that the mode or style of approach to a topic has a profound effect upon the success or otherwise of the committee report in terms of Government responses. But 'success' can be measured in other ways and there are a number of examples in the reports discussed in later chapters, of committee recommendations not being adopted by the Government, but subsequent changes of policy emerging after a lapse of time, coinciding with the select committee recommendations. This 'delayed drop' phenomenon is discussed at greater length in Chapter 10.

In some of the investigations on environmental issues, committees exhibit more than one dominant mode and examples of the four main modes are identified below.

The select committee as advocate and agenda setter

To establish policy where none previously existed or to raise issues of an administrative or practical nature which had not been considered by Government is a legitimate role for select committees. It is a function which many of those giving evidence to committees would utilise in their argument. In the field of environmental policy making the prime example of such an instance in the 1983-87 parliament was the investigation undertaken by the Trade and Industry Committee, entitled The Wealth of Waste, which was concerned to establish the argument that waste disposal and the recycling of discarded industrial material was a legitimate issue of environmental concern, and one on which there should be clearly defined policy (see Chapters 6 and 7).

The Wealth of Waste report (HC 640, 1984) was able to establish the poor record of the UK in waste recycling from both industrial and domestic sources, and to challenge the then view of Government that it was entirely a matter for commercial judgement as to whether the recycling of material was economic or not. In effect, it established the case that there were environmental costs and benefits as well as commercial ones to which the Government should address itself.

In a range of products from paper, glass, rubber and metals British industry did less well than its European counterparts and the committee successfully challenged the Government's statement that it "has not thought it appropriate to develop a national policy for [recycling industrial waste] for the section as a whole". Nor had it identified any department or minister to take overall control of this policy area, despite evidence from ministers in the DOE and their counterparts in the Department of Trade and Industry (DTI) to the effect that both thought they had the 'lead' role. But the resistance of industrialists and trade association witnesses to the proposal that other than commercial considerations should be relevant, suggested a tendency in the relatively closed policy community of the DTI and its contacts, to see the matter only in the mutually shared values of that group.

The success of this select committee enquiry was essentially in establishing a new policy agenda: the environmental aspect of waste reclamation and recycling.

To ask, as writers such as Hogwood and Gunn (1984) do, whether it is the role of policy analysts to seek to place on the policy agenda issues which are not currently receiving attention, may also imply arguments for changing political institutions or for the distribution of power - an underlying theme of the whole debate about select committees and their role vis-a-vis the Executive. For example Stringer and Richardson (1980) call for more open government in the UK on the grounds that more attention would be paid by the Government to the identification of problems, if these were subject to critical review from outside the government apparatus. The agenda setting role in this instance justifies the proposition and despite a small input from environmental pressure groups, established positive Government responses to four out of ten recommendations (see Table 9, p 120).

The report produced Government statements which explicitly recognised the need to assign a value to the environment and to the energy conservation element of recycling including a promise to consider implementing new powers under Sections 12/14 of the Control of Pollution Act 1974 (Waldegrave, 1984). Whilst no firm Government initiatives were forthcoming from The Wealth of Waste investigation, there is ample evidence that the agenda had been expanded irrevocably both for industrialists and for Government policy makers.

The select committee as analyst and evaluator

When members of a select committee take on the role of policy analysts, they face some problems which affect the mode of an enquiry. They must distinguish between failures of implementation, which it is the purpose of monitoring to avoid, and failure of policy. In the former, the mode may be a challenging or critical one as we have seen above, but in the latter circumstances a more evaluative stance may be productive, especially where the wider policy community confirms that policy itself is defective. It is here that a pluralistic approach, as discussed in Smith and Cantley (1985) may be effective.

The Environment Committee's examination of Part II of the Wildlife and Countryside Act 1981 is an example of a select committee investigation in the mode of analysing and evaluating policy. This measure when passed was characterised by the Government as "the most important piece of countryside legislation this century" (Department of the Environment, 1983). Its acknowledged aim was to resolve the conflicting interests of wildlife conservation and the needs of agriculture, and by the use of the 'voluntary principle' to provide protection for sites of special scientific interest and generous financial compensation to affected landowners. That the Act had a difficult birth is attested by the fact that it produced over 200 hours of debate and over 1,000 amendments were tabled (Hansard, 1981).

By 1984, however, there was a growing acceptance within the policy community that it was flawed, and that a loophole in its provisions was being exploited. A number of aspects of the policy were not working. In a survey of local authorities conducted by Council for the Preservation of Rural England (CPRE) only 8 of the 39 English counties regarded the policy mechanisms open to them as adequate for the preservation of the landscape and conservation of wildlife habitats (Council for the Protection of Rural England, 1984). The Royal Society for the Protection of Birds' (RSPB) evidence to the committee concentrated on Part II of the Act, "parts of which are in most urgent need of remedial action" (Royal Society for the Protection of Birds, 1984, p 208).

The purpose of the committee's enquiry, explicitly set out by the chair, was to analyse this failure, to evaluate the Act's effectiveness or lack of it, and to propose some remedies:

> As written submissions began to flood in, it became apparent that Part II is to us the crux of the legislation as it is concerned with the conservation of our natural heritage. Our sense of urgency, fostered by the need to deal as soon as possible with the 'loopholes' led us to put aside Parts I and III and to focus on the central issue.

In particular there has been considerable public anxiety recently about the so called loopholes in Sections 28 and 29. There is unanimous agreement, including by the Government, that this problem is in especially urgent need of resolution. However, we have concluded that there are other weaknesses in the Act which also require action. (HC 6, vol 1, p xi)

It is clear from the tone of this report that any sense of challenge to Government policy is mitigated by an acceptance on behalf of Government that change is required, and the evidence of quasi-governmental bodies such as the Nature Conservancy Council (NCC) whose memoranda made clear that despite originally welcoming the provisions of Part II, a number of shortcomings in the legislation had become evident "at an early stage" (Nature Conservancy Council, 1984, para 2.6).

This allows the committee mode to be collaborative in evaluating not only the nature of the loopholes but the measures required to close them.   This evaluative stance highlighted a number of specific points which the Government acknowledged in its response (Cmnd 9522), and which it undertook to act upon.

Thus the interests of many 'stakeholders' in the policy, each with varying criteria for success in their own terms, have been tabled. These may contribute to the effectiveness of the committee's eventual report in modifying Government policy, since the department's own evaluation process is unlikely to have scanned such a wide field of interest. Since implementation is undertaken by a wide range of semi-autonomous or voluntary agencies, only a select committee is likely to expose conflicting or varying values among stakeholders: another factor which makes it less easy for departments of state to equivocate.

This report is an example of a committee taking up a specific inadequacy in legislation monitored by the whole of the wider policy community including the pressure groups, the conservationists, the bodies operating on behalf of the Government and the department of state itself.   Indeed, it appears that the committee investigation was seen as a helpful mechanism to bring together this monitoring of the effectiveness of the Act, the evaluation of the shortcomings and support for new proposals.

In its response to the committee report the Government accepts the committee's assessment of the problem and as a means of remedying shortcomings supports a private member's Bill:

The Government is therefore supporting a clause in the Wildlife and Countryside (Amendment) Bill designed to give statutory effect to ensure a reasonable balance between forestry and conservation. (Cmnd 9522, p 13)

The Government accepts this recommendation and recognises there is a growing body of opinion in favour of broadening the scope of Section 43 of the Act. The committee's recommendation in this respect has been paralleled by the inclusion of a clause to that effect in the current Wildlife and Countryside (Amendment) Bill. (Cmnd 9522, p 15)

The Government agrees that the financial guidelines should be reviewed to take account of the committee's points. ... The Government recognises the force of some of the criticisms that have been made of the guidelines, particularly about their complexity and it accepts the committee's recommendation that a review of their content and presentation would be timely. (Cmnd 9522, p 17)

Another committee which adopted the role of evaluator and analysor in its approach to an environmental issue was the Committee for Welsh Affairs. Its report on coastal pollution in Wales is published as HC 101 (1985).

The burden of the investigation was concerned with monitoring the apparent conflicts in policies concerning the exploitation of Welsh beaches for tourism, leisure and recreation, with those which exploit coastal waters for sewage disposal, the control of agricultural waste and the quality of water. The evident conflicts in the roles of the Welsh Water Authority, the Welsh Office and the Ministry of Agriculture, Fisheries and Foods was a prime topic as was the question as to who should have responsibility for monitoring water quality at beaches used for recreation. The local authorities argued that they should have statutory powers to undertake sea water sampling on a regular basis. They referred to the potential conflict of interest resulting from a situation in which the water authority, the major sewage polluter of beaches, also had responsibility for water quality monitoring.

That the critical recommendations of the Committee for Welsh Affairs were responded to by the Welsh Water Authority, and were largely in a tone of acceptance and concurrence with shortcomings in the legislation and interorganisational cooperation is significant. Replies make clear that both the Government and its agents in the field of sewage disposal would collaborate in the terms of the evaluative comments from the committee, with an emphasis on further research, new initiatives and more attention to cooperation between local authorities and statutory undertakers. Witnesses in the enquiry had been primarily concerned to analyse the technical nature of these shortcomings and to assess the need for improvement. Far from seeing the report and the tone of the committee's approach as being a challenge or criticism of policy, the work undertaken in the investigation was seen essentially as helpful and as a contribution to finding new solutions. The investigations exposed some basic problems of evaluation, particularly in the lack of agreement on criteria or indicators and the inherent danger that very specific indicators, used in scientific evidence can be at the expense of more qualitative measures.

The select committee as mediator

The considerable public concern which arose from two DOE draft circulars on green belts and land for housing took ministers and officials by surprise (Department of the Environment, 1984b; see commentary pp 84-94).

The Environment Select Committee stepped into the argument explicitly to resolve the apparently irreconcilable interests of developers and conservationists, both of which groups had seen the draft circulars as strengthening their interests. The committee report isolates the issue and sets the mode at the outset:

> Were the circulars all things to all men? [sic] ... If so ... the result might be a system of piecemeal planning by appeal. This we would consider most undesirable. (HC 275, 1984, p xi)

Thus the committee was attempting to reconcile the apparently irreconcilable; demand for development competes with the desire for conservation of the environment. With pressure for new housing development particularly in the South Eastern Region there are on one side volume house builders needing land situated in environments in which people wish to live and to buy houses. On the other side are conservationists and existing residents usually strongly opposed to development on green field sites.

The select committee correctly perceived that the arguments between builders, planners and environmental groups over the need for new land for housing had become increasingly heated and the draft circulars had not contributed to a resolution of the issue.

The select committee's first task was a succinct analysis of the problem:

> To defend green belts there has to be sufficient land for housing available elsewhere. To promote urban housing there have to be defensible green belts. (HC 275, 1984)

Thus the tone or mode of this enquiry is clearly seen to be prioritising policy objectives and at the same time attempting to mediate between conflicting legitimate interests. It pinpoints the failure of the department to recognise the conflict. Pointing out that the two circulars are complementary and interdependent, the committee defines the cause of the conflict:

> The green belt circular attempts to reinforce presumptions against development in certain areas. The land for housing circular attempts to encourage development in remaining areas other than national parks and areas of outstanding natural beauty but the failure to make this distinction has muddled the debate and is a central issue in our report. (HC 275, 1984)

There is subjective evidence that the minister and the DOE actively welcomed the committee's role in defusing and clarifying this issue which had become a major debate within the local government and wider policy environment (Rossi, 1987). Indeed, the Government response (HC 635 1983/4) indicated that it was very helpful to ministers in considering the way forward and the text of the substantive circulars reflected important suggestions which the committee had proposed.

The subsequent substantive circulars (Department of the Environment, 1984b), amended to take account of the committee's report, succeeded in meeting the objectives: they represent an important example of the select committee in a mediating role at the same time analysing and clarifying policy objectives in a way which the department itself had signally failed to do.

Another example of the Environment Committee in mediating mode was provided in the report on historic buildings and ancient monuments (HC 146 1986/87), a topic in which a complex range of statutory and semi-autonomous bodies were actively involved. Relationships between the DOE, English Heritage, the Historic

Buildings and Monuments Commission, the church and a large list of private owners and local authorities were complicated by varying financial and grant-aiding systems and by conflicts concerning responsibilities and differences of approach.

The select committee's attempt to rationalise these issues was acknowledged by the secretary of state who characterised their report as "a useful pulling together of views from all the major interest groups in the heritage field". He added:

> It has provided a most valuable starting point and a rich quarry of ideas and data for the refinement and development of policy towards the heritage, and is likely to remain valid for this purpose for a considerable time to come. (HC 268, 1988)

This would appear to be tantamount to admitting that the select committee's report was to be used as the prime policy planning document for future departmental initiatives - a considerable achievement even if only a percentage of the recommendations were accepted initially.

The select committee as challenger and monitor

The Environment Committee reports which received the most substantial national discussion during the parliament of 1983-87 and which brought together a complex array of technical and scientific evidence, were also those which attracted the biggest volume of anxious public opinion and drew pressure group concern to the committee's attention.

They were the reports on the destructive effects of acid rain and the storage of radioactive waste. In both these reports the committee and many of those who presented evidence were acting in a mode of open challenge to ministers, highly critical of policy - or the lack of it - and at the same time forecasting and monitoring the repercussions of not pursuing a vigorous and coherent strategy for the protection of the environment from both these late-twentieth century phenomena (see case study discussion, pp 94-104)

The tone is set in the chair's introduction to the radioactive waste report (HC 191, 1986, p xii):

> It has become apparent to us that far from there being well-defined, publicly debated policy on the creation,

management and disposal of radioactive waste, there was confusion and obfuscation among the various organisations entrusted with its care.

Having decided to launch an enquiry, and with public interest intensified by Sir Frank Layfield's 1987 report on the Sizewell B public enquiry and another report critical of the nuclear industry following a leak of radioactive material on the beaches around Sellafield (Black, 1984), the Environment Committee is frank about what its investigation reveals:

> The more we looked at what was happening in the UK and compared this country's performance with that of other nations, the more our initial, superficial impression was confirmed. In short the UK government and nuclear industry are confused. (HC 191, 1986, p xii)

Frustrated by the evidence of uncertainty and lack of policy direction, the committee cites, from the submissions of its witnesses, on the one hand bold announcements about prospective new disposal sites which are then withdrawn, left hanging in the air or modified ad hoc (HC 191, p xii). On the other hand, a very large proportion of radioactive waste continues to be produced unquestioned and a sequence of different studies shows that the UK is only feeling its way towards a coherent policy. Indeed, as the committee sat, the DOE was engaged in a 'best practical options' study. It was against this background that the committee report to parliament states: "for an issue which is of such public concern, the secretary of state's evidence to us is regrettably inadequate".

This mode of challenge extends to the other bodies involved in the industry and in the development of waste disposal policies. Its report is bluntly critical of organisational responsibilities. In response to the minister's evidence that a review of these issues had recently been undertaken and was a matter of almost constant debate, the committee expressed itself "not convinced" that the lines of responsibility in radioactive waste management were as clear or as straightforward as they could be (HC 191, p cxxi). They demanded that the review be published (see HC 191, recommendation 37). Of the Government's research programme the report says:

> We found at least two areas where research was lacking and needed urgently. These areas appear to have been neglected

because they fall outside the area of immediate policy. This is a regrettably shortsighted approach. (HC 191, 1986, p 1iii)

The forthright declaration of inadequacy of policy is echoed in the second major report, that on acid rain pollution, a topic to which the committee has returned with a persistence unusual in select committee work.

Following its long and detailed 1983/84 report (HC 446), and a strongly argued Government response (Cmnd 9397), the Environment Committee produced a follow-up report in the 1985/86 session (HC 51).   This presented the responses of Government ministers from Norway and West Germany which are the two countries alleged to suffer most from acid rain pollution emanating from the UK. It also included a welcoming response from the EC and others all essentially aligning themselves with the select committee challenge to the Government's policies in this area. In the subsequent parliament of 1987 the attack was to be renewed in an even wider-ranging report on air pollution (HC 270, 1988).

The challenging mode of the first of this series of reports was, it would appear, partly engendered by the resistance which the committee had met in undertaking its enquiry. Sir Hugh Rossi, the committee chair reported later that there had been "great official resistance" not only towards the need for action but also to the acceptance that the emission of invisible gases from British power stations and industry were responsible for environmental damage both to fish and trees, at home and abroad (Rossi, 1988).

The report acknowledges that having started with an open mind, the evidence which members heard was to convince them that the committee should confront the secretary of state with a demand that no further prevarication was acceptable, and that hard financial decisions had to be taken immediately. The Government's pleas that more research was required before decisions were arrived at was, in the committee's words, "to procrastinate".   Similar castigation is reserved for the Central Electricity Generating Board (CEGB) for making virtually no reduction in its SO_2 emissions despite being the major fossil fuel burner in the country.

Thus it is possible to discern in these two committees' investigations a persistent, direct challenge to Government and other agencies in the field. This reinforces critical observations with evidence to support forecasts of the results of further failure to act, and unchallenged scientific evidence of the results of current policy stances: in other words, monitoring performance and forecasting outcomes.

The particular characteristic of this mode of proceeding is the tendency to reflect the opposition or argument of the wider policy community, not only to current Government policy and action, but to the 'performance' in a wider sense of the whole range of actors and organisations involved. In the examples above, the committee's ability to examine witnesses from foreign governments - and subsequently to publish their responses to the report - takes the international flavour of the issue to the heart of the otherwise 'local' nature of the argument between the Executive and the legislature: a reinforcement of the fact that the Government, in these issues, faced challenge from the international community, and needed to defend more than a domestic record. The evidence of the reports discussed in this study suggests that whilst the 'challenge' mode is unlikely to result in immediate acceptance of major recommendations, there is a tendency for policy changes to appear incrementally and unacknowledged at a later date. This is discussed in Chapter 10.

Issue type

One of the factors which may determine how influential select committee investigations are in securing policy change is the nature of the issue which is examined in particular enquiries. One purpose of this and subsequent chapters will be to differentiate these types and to test the hypothesis that some may be inherently more likely to achieve success than others.

It is important, in defining issue type to distinguish the concept from the quite different point made by one committee chair, quoted earlier, that he deliberately avoided topics which were controversial in party terms or would, in any case, be bound to be debated fully on the floor of the House (Rossi, 1985a). This book is not concerned with the political volatility or sensitivity of the issue in hand, where measurement will be to do with voting strength. Rather, it is about testing the importance of content, irrespective of sectional prejudice.

However, in this connection it is well to recall the allied comment of Sir Hugh Rossi, that his committee would want to take on subjects which busy ministers were unlikely to have the time to grasp in the requisite detail (Rossi, 1987). It is also the case that in promoting enquiries whose content is on the frontiers of technical knowledge, the scientific witnesses and the complex nature of the evidence represents, in several of the reports considered here, some kind of titanic struggle between the experts called to give evidence by the various groups within the policy community.

On the pages of select committee investigative reports, the Friends of the Earth and Greenpeace challenge the CEGB or British Nuclear Fuels Ltd (BNFL) on an entirely esoteric battleground determined by the nature of nuclear physics. Departmental experts are pitted against the specialist advisers for industrial associations and from lawyers at a level of professional knowledge, arcane in the extreme, concerning the administration of planning law or the management of historic buildings. The economic value of scrap metal is at the heart of the debate between the DTI, the representatives of manufacturing industry and the energy conservation lobby. It is the nature of these disputations which determines issue type. What then are the main types of issue - the core of the arguments before the members of the committees?

In the case of the ten enquiries on environmental topics it is possible to distinguish three main issue types, the characteristics of which are distinctive one from another. They are:

● administrative topics;

● technical/scientific topics;

● economic topics.

In defining subject-matter in this way (see Table 2) it is not suggested that each is exclusively concerned with or limited to that material. For example, the report on radioactive waste clearly has complex administrative problems associated with it and involves interdepartmental and interorganisational bureaucratic processes. It also has important economic consequences for the nuclear industry and for environmental policy. Nevertheless, in terms of the debate in which the topic was argued in the select committee, the recommendations to Government and the nature of the conflicts between witnesses for the various groups who gave evidence, it was essentially a technical/scientific subject and the coinage of the arguments which the committee was attempting to deploy was scientific in content. In other words, it was the questioning of the scientific premises of national policy which the committee was undertaking and it would be in those terms that the argument would be won or lost.

By the same token the report *Planning: appeals, call-in and major public enquiries* (HC 181, 1986) is categorised as an administrative topic on the grounds that it is essentially the administration of policy which is under scrutiny. Much of planning policy is conducted and modified in departmental circulars, ministerial directives and codes of guidance, the standard traffic of central/local bureaucratic relations. The matters at issue for the select committee were, for the most part, concerned with procedures for appeal, the process of 'call-in' where the secretary of state intervenes, and the conduct of major planning enquiries. Other recommendations dealt with the conduct of local authority procedures, the need to cut down delays and the powers of inspectors. Much of the evidence was directed at the need to make these processes work more effectively rather than to comment on the substantive policy issues underlying them. Indeed, the committee commented adversely on the tendency for policy debate to be staged at major public enquiries such as the Sizewell B power station planning enquiry, rather than in parliament and made clear that its main concern was that the system of enquiries and appeals could be made faster and more efficient (HC 181, 1986). The Government's response included the announcement of new procedural rules to speed up the process (Cm 43, 1986, App 1).

Table 2:   Select committee reports by issue type

Report	Issue type
Green belt and land for housing	Administrative
Acid rain	Technical/scientific
Wealth of waste	Economic
Wildlife and Countryside Act Part II	Administrative
Coastal pollution in Wales	Technical/scientific
Radioactive waste	Technical/scientific
Planning: appeals, call-in and major public enquiries	Administrative
Pollution of rivers and estuaries	Technical/scientific
Historic buildings and ancient monuments	Administrative
Caravan Sites Act 1968	Administrative

It is for these reasons and for the purposes of this study that the select committee investigation is designated 'administrative', and the same approach has been applied to other committee enquiries considered here, to isolate the main theme or leitmotiv as accepted by all participants to the investigation. On this basis, all ten of the reports considered in this thesis have been categorised as falling into one of the three issue types identified as shown in Table 2.

In defining the nature of issues as a measure it will be argued in Chapter 10 that when there is a discussion as to whether the concept has relevance in a wider context, there may be different definitions to be established than those established here.

A matrix for measurement

Three separate factors present in a select committee enquiry have been established, based upon observation of those committees and enquiries dealing with environmental policy (listed in Table 3, p 80) which may have a bearing upon the degree of success such committees achieve in modifying policy or effecting policy change.

To summarise, these factors are:

● the point in the policy process at which the select committee report attempts intervention (intervention);

● the nature or 'mode' of enquiry pursued by the committee (committee mode);

● the nature of the issue under scrutiny (issue type).

The next step in the process is to place these three variables into some form of matrix through which it may be possible to identify whether any of the factors listed above can be shown to be linked to success more than others, or, as is more likely, whether some combination of the separate factors registers more successful outcomes than others. Such a matrix is essentially a framework for organising an understanding of what happens and what combination of circumstance produces successful responses (see Figure 5).

Figure 5: The matrix for assessment of committee effectiveness based on issue type, mode and intervention point

Committee:		Topic:		
Committee mode:	Policy process intervention:		Issue type:	

Input score and citations

Ministers and government departments	Quangos and official agencies	Local authorities	Self-interest groups	Pressure groups	Independent experts

Government responses to recommendations

Positive acceptance and action	General agreement	Acceptance for consideration	Neutral comment	Rejection

It is not, at this stage, intended to argue a prescriptive case; to say that if, for example, a committee wants to make maximum change, it should first choose a scientific or an administrative issue, and then conduct its enquiry in a particular way, having first made sure that the subject was at the commencement of its career in the parliamentary policy process. Rather, it has already been pointed out above that the reality of political activity is often subjective, irrational and motivated by a wide range of imperatives. The value of a theoretical framework of this kind is its tendency to retrospective 'rationality' in a process which is essentially incremental and which may owe more to opportunism, ideology - and even chance - than to pre-ordained 'good practice'.

A matrix of the kind illustrated in Figure 5 would also allow a further dimension of measurement to be attempted.

The sources of evidence

This study has set out to quantify all the inputs to the committee enquiry; to list the interest or locus of witnesses and the origin of technical papers, appendices, and memoranda in terms of the groups represented within the wider policy community. These groupings are identified in six categories thus:

- ministers and government departments;

- quangos and other official agencies;

- local authorities;

- self-interest groups;

- pressure groups;

- independent experts.

Some explanation of the basis of these groupings is required. In allocating each input to one of the above categories bodies such as the CEGB, the NCC and English Heritage, who have either a statutory responsibility for the implementation of official policy, or are operating as a nationalised commercial enterprise or in some other quasi-governmental role in the carrying out of policy, are differentiated from formal ministerial or departmental inputs. In one case, the identification with official policy was such that, it was the Welsh Water Authority which responded formally to the report on coastal pollution in Wales (HC 01, 1985) on behalf of the Welsh Office. In another (HC 146, 1986/87), English Heritage responded to the Environment Committee's recommendations in addition to the DOE. Nevertheless, in these instances it is possible to detect a distinction between policy and implementation; a degree of differentiation of response as between those in control of purse-strings and those charged with the practical implementation of legislative provisions.

It is also necessary to make a distinction between various kinds of lobbying organisations and pressure groups. The rather wide definition proposed by Lindblom does not seem adequate:

> We mean by interest group activities all interactions through which individuals and private groups not holding government authority, seek to influence policy, together with those policy-influencing interactions of government officials that go well beyond the direct use of their authority. (Lindblom, 1980)

Lindblom's definition does not allow for the basic difference between self-interested groups whose aim is to pursue sectional - and usually economic - ends on the one hand, and those which seek to promote a shift in values or practices. Potter (1961) provides a demarcation between: "sectional interests and shared values". He suggests that the former purport to speak "in defence" of their members and the latter to "promote" the causes which reflect the attitudes of their members. Potter readily admits that there are borderline cases and even this definition would give rise to some problems in the context of those giving evidence to select committees, especially on matters of environmental protection.

Moran (1985) and Cawson (1982) distinguish between functional groups and preference groups: the first created by the economic structure, for example representing capital and labour, the second arising from free association between individuals linked by common attitudes, positions or tasks. The comment of Stewart (1958) is relevant here since he draws attention to those 'cause' groups not admitted to governmental consultation. It is one of the developing features of select committee enquiries that many such groups find a platform in the heart of Westminster, which they would not be granted either by the Government or the civil service.

Most commentators would allow that what is here termed the self-interest groups, often with regular and bureaucratised relations with government departments, need to be weighed differently from those voluntary bodies with a disinterested 'cause', which are here termed 'pressure groups'. For the purposes of categorising evidence to select committees on environmental issues, therefore, self-interest groups are those with a commercial or financial stake in the issue under discussion, and in this paper have included bodies such as the CBI, trade associations, land-owners, individual companies and the National Farmers Union (NFU). Pressure groups have encompassed voluntary associations with a moral or ideological identification with an issue; bodies representing a point of view of a wide grouping of individuals, such as Greenpeace, the Friends of the Earth, the RSPB and groups with a campaigning role who seek to represent specific common interests of members and to influence Government. These groups may range from political activists with considerable influence to small groups or local coalitions in defence of local amenity; from the financially powerful direct action of Greenpeace, to the Claygate village residents association.

The distinction drawn in this book is between a self-protective or disinterested concern for policy change and a commercial or financial interest in the outcome of Government action.

Other evidence has come from a group of academic or specialist sources with a professional interest in research, or professional expertise ranging from individual scientists and teachers to internationally-known institutes, laboratories and universities.

An attempt will be made to equate the weight of evidence produced from these separate sources with the frequency with which committee reports have cited such evidence in framing the recommendations to Government. Is it, for example, the case that evidence from one of the six listed sources is more predominant than others, and is there a correlation between the volume of such evidence and the citations it produces? Does the number of recommendations accepted by Government have any relationship to the volume of evidence and citation which went into the framing of the recommendations? These questions will be examined in a later chapter and the analysis will rely upon the matrix shown in Figure 5 (p 71).

Having set up a machinery for analysis, it is necessary to address other, pertinent questions which arise. What is meant by 'success' in this context? If it can be shown that there is a sound basis for assessing the factors which determine committee success or failure in the policy area of the environment, is it robust enough to apply in other areas of policy or to the work of other, quite different select committees?

As we move on to an examination of these and other issues it is worth returning to the proposition of one of the commentators on the early work of the new select committee system. In summing up the comprehensive seminar held by Strathclyde University (reviewed in Chapter 2) the editor suggests that the new system and the activity of select committees has changed the policy process irrevocably (Hill, 1984).

The underlying argument in this chapter has, on the contrary, led to the view that it is not the policy process which is changed but rather that it is the point at which the committee report intervenes in that process, which is significant: that success or failure may be more to do with the point of impact than with the process itself. To put the question a different way, if a select committee engages with a policy issue at the point when it is being defined and quantified by the responsible department, will the committee's proposals influence the policy outcome more than if its engagement is at the point when it is being implemented or when a long-standing piece of policy is being reviewed and reassessed?

There follows a practical examination of the efficacy of the propositions in this chapter. That select committees have established a role which Governments cannot ignore and are an important part of the complex parliamentary mechanisms available to back-bench members and external actors seeking to influence policy, is widely acknowledged. They are not the most significant part of that complexity but as Giddings (1985) remarked, they are there "a cloud no bigger than a man's hand ...', which is a suitable image from which to proceed to an examination in more detail of environmental policy and the role which select committees have played in its formation during the parliament of 1983-87. By examining the policy related to environmental protection and analysing in detail select committee evidence and reports - and the responses of government departments - the concepts outlined in this chapter can begin to be applied and their validity assessed.

six

THE ENVIRONMENT AS A POLICY AREA

Introduction

The emergence of 'the environment' as a coherent arena for policy and action in British politics has been slow, spasmodic and incremental. The notions of what were later to become subsumed into a broad concept of 'green politics' stem largely from the conflicts between industrial development and environmental conservation, between the demand for natural resource exploitation and the preservation of amenity. Much of the initiative and public pressure to promote policy change has come from outside the political community with origins in America and Western Europe as often as in the UK. Governments have, on the whole, been reactive rather than originators: it has been academics and lobbyists who have proposed interconnections between accelerating industrialisation, rapid population growth, widespread malnutrition, depletion of non-renewable resources and a deteriorating environment (Forrester, 1971).

Propagandists such as Ralph Nader in the USA and the emergence of the Green Party in West Germany testify to the international nature of threats to the ecology of the world as well as to the transnational nature of modern capitalism.

Various commentators have suggested that these issues emerged in some kind of spontaneous explosion of public concern (Allaby, 1971), but a careful study of the last four decades gives a different impression. As a political issue or area of public concern, the emergence of an environmental agenda has been more of a gradual imposition on the consciousness of Whitehall and Westminster policy makers (Brookes et al, 1976). In a contents count of *The Times* newspaper Brookes and his colleagues demonstrate a much slower dawning, and a more complex process by which the mass media and the public awareness of these issues emerged. By counting the growth of news items, letters and features from 1953 to 1973, they suggest that the new environmentalism in Britain follows closely on the anti-war and anti-pollution movements in the USA in the 1960s. They trace a cumulative pattern whereby as the coverage of specific news items increases, it becomes easier to accept that there exists an underlying problem and not just a series of smaller isolated incidents or issues. Thus the media slowly began to place individual incidents, public enquiries or protests on ecological matters into a wider framework of environmental awareness which itself assumed the nature of a topic with continuing interest for the media and the general public. In the serious daily press 'environment correspondents' appeared during the later 1970s.

Three phases of debate

Whilst it is in concern over the seemingly endless exploitation of the world's physical resources that the origins of the environmental lobby lie, it is the political, social and economic conflicts which arise when the demand for more resources impinges on less material aspirations which go to form the political agenda. Expressed as 'quality of life', or desecration of communities, arguments may centre on new motorways, reservoirs, mineral extraction or airport noise and expansion (Gregory, 1971).

This represents a change in the nature of the debate since the 1960s. The early phase was indeed to do with the global threat to the whole of mankind in the using up of the world's resources, but in Britain, the issues have emerged as a more specific concern for controls on publicly-sponsored expansion of industrial and nationalised concerns. Issues such as the construction of nuclear power stations, the location of the third London airport and the building of motorways have generated widespread opposition and local campaigns to 'save the natural environment'. In the third and latest phase, the ground of the argument has shifted again with an emphasis on the long-term effects of new technology, nuclear energy and chemical pollution, threats to future generations and to eco-systems and wildlife habitats. Recent apprehensions of the destruction of the ozone layer and consequent 'global warming' are perhaps the most vivid examples of the articulation of these issues on the public consciousness.

What kind of picture emerges in governmental response to these issues? Some commentators argue that environmental policy under successive Conservative Governments has been narrowly focussed and selective, designed to appeal to partisan interests mainly located in southern, suburban and rural England (Blowers, 1987). But it is possible to respond that as the various directives of the EC are implemented so there will be a transformation of British policy away from pragmatic regulation to environmental quality objectives and standards.   Policies for environmental control, endorsed at the international level will severely reduce the ability of national governments to pursue independent environmental policies.

In Britain, the ideology which has proclaimed the virtues of the market has, conversely, produced a debate on the need to preserve the heritage; the very stridency of the argument for free markets has produced a reaction in favour of constraint.   It may be said that the overall effect of the Conservative Governments' approach to the environment has been to nurture that debate to the point where the environment is now a significant issue in national politics, with a permanent place on the agenda and attended by a substantial and widening policy community.   That Mrs Thatcher's successor should establish a 'heritage' ministry as one of the first additions to his 1992 Cabinet gives some credibility to that argument.

Against this background of policy development an examination of the way in which environmental problems have emerged within the select committee system is needed, and how committees have dealt with them in their monitoring of Government and departmental performance. The next part of the argument deployed in this study is based upon the ten major committee reports produced in the second Conservative administration of Mrs Thatcher's premiership for 1983-87, all dealing with the evolving environmental issues discussed above, and seeks to understand how the interests involved and the committees themselves have been instrumental in the evolution of policy.   Three of the most significant committee investigations are examined in detail in the case studies which follow.

Select committees and environmental issues 1983-87

Throughout the parliamentary sessions from 1983 to 1987 there is a consistent thread of work by back-bench MPs in a number of select committees touching upon policies for the protection of the environment, the prevention of pollution, and preservation of historic heritage and the natural habitat: a range of topics which might loosely be called 'environmental issues'. It is an area of public policy which is at once highly scientific and technical in content, profoundly bound up with modern industrial processes and at the same time attracting a passionate interest from a small but articulate and largely middle class community of pressure groups.

Equally, many of the issues have important implications for industrial and commercial interests. The deleterious effects of acid rain, the disposal of toxic wastes and radioactive waste by-products are matters which have a direct effect on the costs of manufacturing processes. They attract powerful voices to the debate.

The Government's approach to the green belt and the release of land for housing is of vital concern to the builders and developers whose own organised interest representation reaches to the centre of power and influence. That a number of departmental select committees have launched enquiries in this general policy area has produced a new and potentially expanding arena in which these conflicting interests can fight their case and bid for the ear of parliament and the policy establishment. The resulting series of select committee reports and the Government replies (see Table 3) range over a wide field and have produced both administrative and substantive changes in policy, positive responses within ministries, debates in the House and on the whole, in the view of many commentators, a collaborative and progressive advance in the public interest. The following pages will examine the extent of the trend and by using three of the reports as case studies illustrate the way in which select committees have dealt with the evidence before them and the Government's response to their recommendations.

The work in this field has been mainly in the Environment Committee, the Trade and Industry Committee and the committees on Welsh and Scottish affairs in the case of regional issues. In all, more than a dozen major enquiries have been undertaken and have resulted in responses either by way of special reports or command papers (see Table 3 below).

Table 3: Select committee reports on environmental topics published during the parliament of 1983-87

Select committee	Subject of report	Sessional no.	HC no.	Reply by gov't
Environment	Green belt/ land for housing	1st 83/4	HC 275	HC 635
Environment	Acid rain	4th 83/4	HC 446 Vol I/II	Cmd 997
Environment	Acid rain (follow-up)	1st Spec 85/6	HC 51	-
Trade and Industry	The wealth of waste	4th 83/4	HC 640	HC 321
Environment	Wildlife and Countryside Act, Part II	1st 84/5	HC 6 Vol I/II	Cmnd 9522
Welsh Affairs	Coastal pollution in Wales	1st 85/6	HC 101	HC 401
Environment	Radioactive waste	1st 85/6	HC 191 HC 211	Cmnd 9852
Environment	Planning: appeals, call-in and major public enquiries	5th 85/6	HC 181	Cm 43
Environment	Pollution of rivers and estuaries	3rd 86/7	HC 183	HC 543
Environment	Historic buildings and ancient monuments	1st 86/7	HC 146	HC 268
Environment	Caravan Sites Act 1968	3rd 84/5	HC 414	

In some cases formal debates in the House have been staged in addition to adjournment debates prompted by back benchers. That there has been such a constructive relationship with Government on these issues, especially in the Environment Committee, is perhaps mainly due to a wish to avoid the kind of controversial political issue which would be likely to bring committee and department into conflict. The decision to avoid controversy was explicit. The committee chair, Sir Hugh Rossi has explained:

> we decided, as an act of conscious policy, not to become involved in topics which are the subject of major political controversy or which are likely to be debated fully on the floor of the House in any event. Instead we decided to identify and concentrate on areas of public concern where the political parties had not defined their attitudes and in which it appeared that ministers had not much time to investigate in depth for themselves. (Rossi, 1987)

Sir Hugh persuaded his committee that in this way they would enhance their prospects of producing unanimous all-party reports which would thereby carry conviction and influence the decision-making processes. It was this approach which led members of the committee, in their major enquiries in this period, into the previously somewhat neglected broader environmental issues.

Not all committees fared so well. The House of Commons Liaison Committee which is made up of the chairs of all departmental select committees reported to the House on the way in which the system was operating, in April 1985 (HC 363, 1985). This document contained brief summaries from the chair of each select committee and it is clear that not all took the same view as Sir Hugh Rossi. In the first five years of the new committee system some 275 reports were produced but only on four occasions were reports debated on substantive motions in the House. Many others were touched upon in the course of normal parliamentary business, and there were numerous occasions on which committee reports provided useful background or were mentioned in matters before the House. The chair of the Liaison Committee complains that the debating time allotted in the House by the Government's business managers is too modest (HC 363, 1985).

This overall picture contrasts markedly with the performance of the Environment Committee. Sir Hugh believes that his policy of 'non-confrontation' has been justified by the results both during that period and subsequently:

> Two Government circulars on planning have been issued taking the recommendations of our first report fully into account. Each of our next three reports was debated separately on the floor of the house evoking positive Government responses and consequential action. Our fifth report in the period was implemented in a private member's Bill supported by the Government, all but one clause of which was based upon our recommendations. (HC 363, 1985)

The chosen subjects of the Environment Commmittee, although possibly not controversial in a party political sense, were certainly matters of vigorous debate in the Whitehall policy community among affected interest groups and local authorities.

For example the first report in session 1983/84 on green belt and land for housing (HC 275, 1984) was sparked by the issuing of two draft circulars on these subjects from the DOE in the summer and autumn of 1983 which were subsequently withdrawn amidst much controversy between planners, conservationists and developers, with particular reference to inner cities. The committee decided to assist in the consultation process started by the department and to play a major role in the taking and sifting through of evidence from interested parties. Over a three month period the committee saw 23 separate groups of witnesses and received over 100 written memoranda. It is clear that the substantive circulars subsequently issued by the DOE had been redrafted in the light of the committee's recommendations (Department of the Environment, 1984b).

Equally positive results flowed from the committee's report on the effects of acid rain (HC 446, 1984), on the operation of Part II of the Wildlife and Countryside Act 1981 (HC 6, 1984) and on further reports dealing with radioactive waste, planning appeals, pollution of rivers and estuaries and the care of ancient monuments, which were produced in subsequent sessions of parliament.

It remains true that despite this series of committee reports highlighting environmental problems, the whole subject of environmental conservation and the dangers of pollution remained during the second Thatcher parliament a marginal issue of limited concern. However early in the following parliament, the whole complex of pollution issues and ecological threat exploded on to the political scene in a major way; 'green politics' became a theme at the top of party agenda throughout British political life. This phenomenon, and the role of select committees in it, are examined in the final chapters of this book.

Meanwhile, by reference to three case studies, the hypothesis for measuring the effectiveness of the select committee system can be tested and the limits of its relevance defined.

seven

THREE CASE STUDIES

Case study I: green belt and land for housing

The complex relationship between central and local government is often regulated and modified by the issue of departmental circulars which can be both directive and advisory. Ministerial circulars, like codes of guidance and consultative documents form part of a complex battery of 'secondary' legislation which can in some circumstances carry the force of common law (Rhodes, 1981). Incremental changes of policy by administrative action frequently occur in this way and the extent of this development is emphasised by the practice of some ministers of issuing draft circulars for comment before enshrining their new proposal in the substantive document.

Such an occasion was the issue by the DOE in 1983 of draft circulars on green belt policy and land for housing which attracted the critical attention of the Environment Select Committee as a result of the widespread debate which ensued (Department of the Environment, 1983). Indeed, the discussion generated was described as 'hysterical' by one commentator (Royal Town Planning Institute, 1984).

The paragraphs on structure and local plans were unexceptional but three paragraphs dealing with guidance on green belt policy caused very considerable concern within the policy community. Some commentators thought them remarkable for their poor timing and political ineptitude (Hall, 1983; Dobson, 1984). On the one hand the circular repeated phrases from earlier circulars (Ministry of Housing and Local Government, 1955) reaffirming that "the essential characteristics of green belts is their permanence, and their protection should be long term", and that "there must continue to be a general presumption against any inappropriate development within them". On the other hand, these assertions of support are followed by a list of circumstances in which the green belts could in fact be made rather impermanent: "broad areas of green belt in structure plans should be altered only exceptionally", and "the inner boundaries of green belts should be carefully drawn so as not to include land which it is unnecessary to keep permanently open for the purpose of the green belt".

A leader in *The Times* put the issue succinctly:

> There is a case for revision of green belt boundaries; considerable tracts of land are neither green (that is, used for agricultural or accessible open space) nor much of a worthwhile girdle. (*The Times*, 8 August, 1983)

Why, asked local authorities if there is no change of policy, is it necessary to issue a new circular? (Cheshire County Council, 1983). The green belt circular was issued shortly after the distribution for consultation of the draft circular *Land for housing*, and the announcement by the Volume House Builders consortium of proposals for 12-15 villages in the South East, of between 5,000 and 7,000 houses each, of which four or five were proposed for green belt sites. In these circumstances it was clear that the minister had in mind some relaxation of existing policy.

The secretary of state took the opportunity of a speech to the Town and Country Planning Association's summer school in 1983 to attempt to put the draft circulars in context. He said:

> I am as committed as any of my predecessors to preserving a strong, clear green belt policy. The essential characteristic of green belts is their permanence and their protection should be long term, but, the growth of green belts creates its own problems. In the last eight years, and mainly since 1979, the London green belt has increased by 45% and is about three times bigger than London itself!

> What the draft circular is primarily about is how the green belt policies that are incorporated in very broad terms in approved structure plans are translated into the detailed boundaries of local plans.

What it says is that in drawing these detailed green belt boundaries they must not be pulled so tightly that there is virtually no room left for development in the future. As our society changes so the planning system must change too in order to retain the confidence on which it depends. Changes in industry, in population and in public attitudes require a response from a planning system. (Jenkin, 1983)

Both circulars were issued during the parliamentary recess, adding to the speculation and debate by local authorities, constituency parties and shire county MPs. The circulars repeat the basic objectives of all green belt land which were set out in Circular 42/55. They are:

- to check the further growth of a large built-up area;

- to prevent neighbouring towns from merging into one another;

- to preserve the special character of a town.

But changes in economic conditions and in the movement of populations have meant a reduction in projected population growth, a substantial reduction in public sector funds available for major growth points and a new emphasis on inner city redevelopment as opposed to outward movement (Dobson, 1984). This attitude is embodied in structure plans and in proposals for the regeneration of inner city areas. Hall (1983) points out that it had never been inherent in green belt policy that such land should either be beautiful or that it should be usable for recreation of any kind. Thus the fact that some of the inner edges of green belts are semi-derelict or waste land has been irrelevant to whether or not such land is serving the green belt purpose.

This point is taken up by the Royal Town Planning Institute (RTPI), in its evidence to the committee:

The RTPI strongly supports the view that properly prepared structure plan green belt policies should only be altered exceptionally. It recognises, however, that the inner boundaries should be drawn carefully and that unnecessary restraint will be self-defeating. (RTPI, 1984)

The suspicion that the secretary of state was seeking to advance a modification of green belt policy as part of a plan to regenerate the house construction industry in the South East led to widespread debate among planners, conservationists and local authorities and to the Environment Select Committee undertaking an enquiry in the spring of 1984 (HC 275, 1984). It provides an example of select committee action in mediating between the pressure groups and industrial self-interest groups, seeking an acceptable formula for policy advance and prioritising conflicting issues and interests. At the same time they challenge the minister and his department to explain an apparent piece of administrative policy making.

The secretary of state had made clear, early in the argument, his concern for the regeneration of the economy and particularly for the house building industry. He said, in a speech to planners, that it was necessary to face the fact that only a small minority of new housing would be built in the inner cities. "There isn't room for large scale development. Most new houses are going to have to be built elsewhere" (Jenkin, 1983). He stressed the Government's economic imperatives by pointing out that over a million people are employed in the construction industry and the increase in house building is one of "the brighter spots" in the economy, he said, "this development must be helped positively by planning authorities" (Jenkin, 1983).

As the committee report makes clear, the planning system is an attempt to reconcile the irreconcilable. Demand for new development competes with the desire for conservation of the environment (HC 275, 1984). Nowhere is this more true than in the housing field with, on the one side, house builders needing land situated in environments in which people will live and, on the other, conservationists and existing residents usually strongly opposed to development on green field sites.

The planning system has to attempt to reconcile the two sides by protecting agricultural land, controlling urban sprawl, yet bringing forward sufficient land to match demand. Volume builders claim the system is failing them (HC 275, 1984). They have argued increasingly that it has become more difficult to obtain sufficient land that can be developed viably to meet what they perceive as the demands of the market. Land prices become more and more crucial a factor as the desire for home ownership expands through all levels of society.

The two draft circulars at the heart of the debate were produced to resolve these competing claims, but also to establish clear policy objectives: the draft circular on house building sets these out as follows:

- the planning system must deliver an adequate and sufficient supply of land suitable for new houses;

- full use must be made of sites within urban areas;

- the planning system must provide for new undeveloped sites;

- all these aims can best be achieved by local planning authorities and house builders working together.

Curiously, the select committee found both sides had welcomed the revised draft circulars; both builders and conservationists found solace in them and planning authorities expected little change in practice. The select committee members asked: Were the circulars all things to all people? Did each side see in the circulars what they wanted to see? If so, have they provided a framework which no-one genuinely understands and on which both sides would call in support? Members felt that the result might be a system of piecemeal planning by appeal and considered this an undesirable outcome (HC 275, 1984).

The select committee took the view that the two circulars were essentially linked. Members stressed three major questions throughout their investigation: do the circulars provide defensible green belts; do they provide a framework within which sufficient land for housing can be identified; do they promote urban regeneration to the maximum possible extent?

The committee investigation was concerned to resolve these conflicting interests and took the view that it was essential to do so in order that the main aims of policy could be maintained: ie the conservation of the natural environment, the improvement of housing standards and of the urban environment. It recognised that the housing circular attempted to encourage development in certain areas other than national parks and conservation areas whilst the green belt circular attempted to reinforce presumptions against development in certain areas.

The committee found that much of the pressure arises in those parts of the country where people want to live, work and enjoy the countryside. Green belts have been set up in most of these critical areas, in many of which are our major urban centres and some of our best agricultural land. The circulars divide these for planning purposes and the report, therefore, makes recommendations to make green belt boundaries sacrosanct, to ensure those boundaries are properly defined, to improve the appearance of designated land, to make sure green belts fulfill their major function of controlling and improving urban development. The committee's recommendations were designed to make planning authorities more responsive to demand, to remove artificial restraints on the planning process, to get builders and planners to cooperate and to maximise urban regeneration.

Evidence was taken from the DOE and from the secretary of state, from local authorities, house builders, conservation organisations and academics. A wide range of pressure groups and other bodies submitted written evidence and the committee, having taken its first evidence in February 1984, published its report in May (HC 275, 1984). The report supports the minister's view that a new circular was necessary especially in that structure plans had largely incorporated green belts as part of wider planning policies and hundreds of local plans were at that time in preparation to define local green belt boundaries. Thus, belatedly, the circular sets green belt policy into the context of structure and local plans, but also recognises the new emphasis on urban regeneration and the changed circumstances of the 1980s so that what had originally been conceived as a way of containing growth was now an essential tool in dealing with the problems of design (Department of the Environment, 1984b). The committee tabled 26 firm recommendations to Government urging the unequivocal establishment of the positive planning role of green belts and presumption against development together with a fourth objective for them: to assist urban regeneration. It was proposed that the longevity of green belts be expressed by the Government as "as far as can be seen ahead".

The committee recommended that the condition of land should not be taken into account when drawing green belt boundaries and that such status should be given to pockets of open land between urban areas within conurbations. The Government was urged to give greater emphasis to countryside enhancement, to create the concept of countryside management, to stimulate local initiatives for the preservation of the green belt including additional funding, together with proposals for rationalising the appeal procedure.

In considering the draft circular on land for housing the committee urged a greater emphasis on planning guides at regional level and the need to ensure that when amenity land is under threat, an acceptable choice is available elsewhere. It went on to recommend a series of actions to encourage local government to assist in the disposal of land to developers, some modifications of the Derelict Land Grant procedure to assist private developers and generally to make the development process easier and the disposal of land more efficient.

The Government's response to the select committee report came in three parts. On the 4th July 1984 the secretary of state provided a written answer in the House of Commons to the first 16 recommendations and revised the text of the draft circulars, largely adopting the comments of the select committee. These drafts were annexed to the official report and published on the day of the written answer (Hansard, 1984).

The second part of the department's response was contained in a letter and memorandum from the secretary of state dated 24th July to the chair of the select committee and was subsequently published as the fifth special report from the committee (HC 635, 1984). This document dealt with the remaining 14 recommendations which are analysed below.

In addition, the secretary of state announced three new initiatives as a result of the committee report. First, he set up an independent body, the Groundwork Foundation, to assist in the formation of local trusts to support green belt policies. Second, he announced proposals for monitoring changes in land use and also to commission consultants to examine methods of surveying the stock of existing land uses as the committee had suggested. Third, he announced a review of the Derelict Land Grant procedures (Jenkin, 1983).

Of 26 specific recommendations, 15 were accepted by Government and significant amendments were made to the text of draft circulars subsequently issued as substantive advice. Seven recommendations were rejected dealing with appeal procedures and the award of costs, and with the disbursement of Derelict Land Grants which the committee had suggested should be 'demand-led'. The committee had also recommended a greater use of urban development corporations (UDCs), a suggestion which the secretary of state declined to accept; it is interesting to note, however, that the 1987 election manifesto of the Conservative Party proposed to institute a series of additional development corporations to deal with the problems of inner city redevelopment and this is perhaps an example of a select committee idea being rejected initially but finding its way on to the wider policy agenda in subsequent years.

Four of the committee's recommendations, although not accepted immediately were to be the subject of further review by the Government, dealing mainly with administrative and procedural issues which the committee had suggested were inhibiting swift development and land disposal (HC 635, 1984).

This select committee investigation demonstrated the committee essentially in the 'analysing' mode, pressing for explanations of administrative instructions and advice, but at the same time mediating and explaining the controversial subject matter and providing a platform for conflicting interest groups. In this sense the committee undertook a valuable intervention in mediating between the interests of volume builders, planning authorities and environmental pressure groups.

The subject under review was essentially the administrative issues surrounding green belt and development policies and the range of inputs included witnesses from government departments, the secretary of state, economic self-interest groups, environmental pressure groups and local planning authorities. Expert independent advice came largely from academic sources. A total of 139 inputs to the committee's deliberations analysed in Table 4 included, in addition to the evidence given by witnesses and replies to questions, memoranda, technical appendices and a substantial number of unpublished memoranda, letters and other documents. This table also analyses the number of times particular sources of evidence were cited in the committee's published report, giving some indication of the use which members made of the material presented to them.

That both local authorities and the volume builders have a direct interest in the practical administration of green belt policy and the release of land for new housing development, was demonstrated by the volume of evidence which came from both sources, and as will be seen by the matrix analysis, they accounted for 62% of all inputs to the committee investigation (see Figure 6 and Table 4 below).

The pressure groups, however, including those with some official functions in the preservation of the green belt achieved a high degree of influence in the shaping of the final recommendations to parliament. The secretary of state's decision in 1984 to issue new draft guidance had aroused concerns from all sides as to his intentions. What can be seen in this example of select committee influence is the mediation of conflicting interests, worked out in a detailed and functional way, bringing the legitimate concerns of both developers and preservationists into a series of recommendations of which the large majority were acceptable to Government.

Table 4: Analysis of inputs and citations in the select committee report on green belts and land for housing (HC 275, Session 1983/84)

	Ministers/ government departments	Quangos/ official agencies	Local authorities	Self-interest groups	Pressure groups	Independent experts
Witnesses examined	12	-	32	11	6	10
Supporting memoranda	3	-	10	4	4	3
Technical appendices	1	-	5	2	2	1
Other written memoranda/ unpublished evidence	0	-	24	-	3	6
Totals	16	-	71	17	15	20
Citations count	34	-	63	27	15	8
Total inputs	50	-	134	44	30	28
	17.5%	-	47.0%	15.5%	10.5%	9.5%

Figure 6: Matrix analysis - green belts and land for housing

Committee: Environment			Topic: Green belts and land for housing		
Committee mode: Analysis and mediator		**Policy process intervention:** Policy implementation monitoring and control	**Issue type:** Administrative		
Input score and citations					
Ministers and government departments	Quangos and official agencies	Local authorities	Self-interest groups	Pressure groups	Independent experts
50	-	134	44	30	28
Government responses to recommendations					
Positive acceptance and action	General agreement	Acceptance for consideration	Neutral comment	Rejection	
7	7	4	2	5	

Note: This framework is utilised for each of the committee investigations examined in this study, showing for each one, the mode and issue type, the intervention point in the policy cycle, and a numerical count of the inputs of evidence and the citation count. Finally, it lists the Government's responses to all the recommendations.

In later chapters it will be possible to compare the matrix analysis of this committee report with others listed in Table 3 (see p 80) and draw some tentative conclusions about the means of measuring committee influence on policy, at the same time defining the limits to quantitative approaches to the question.

Case study II: acid rain

More frequently than in earlier generations, debates which begin in other countries and issues which are continental rather than national in character are forced onto the policy agenda of the British parliament. This is not simply due to British membership of the EC but stems from many factors including advances in communications, the international nature of finance, trade, energy resources and economic interdependence.

Ecological and environmental matters are typically transnational in character. The rise of green politics and of pressure groups in defence of amenity have made pollution a matter of concern in parliaments across the world. The environmental lobby has grown in a generation from a series of fringe pressure groups to a central position in the policy communities in a wide range of governmental activity and capitalistic enterprise (Rivers, 1974).

Such was the context for the Environment Select Committee's interest in the problems and policies associated with acid rain. In 1983 advances in policy and collective action in a number of European nations were going on without the UK, and Britain's contribution to continental eco-damage over a wide area of Scandinavia and Northern Europe was being quantified more precisely than before (Department of the Environment, 1984a). The Government's policy position was explicit:

> Pollution is dealt with by political action, but is explained by science. Science is dynamic and the policies of the other governments must evolve to meet new evidence. What is durable within this framework of change is the Government's overall policy: that action against pollution shall rest on the best scientific evidence, the best technical and economic analysis and the best possible assessment of priorities. (Cmnd 9397, 1984)

The term 'acid rain' was first used in 1872 to describe the atmospheric chemical processes whereby sulphur dioxide, emitted when coal is burnt, falls as sulphuric acid in rain. Today it is used to describe acid deposition, wet, dry and occult - ie mists and fog - caused by a number of pollutants emitted when fossil fuels are burned. The term is both graphic and evocative, thereby readily lending itself to the dynamics of political controversy.

Having achieved nearly 40% reduction in sulphor dioxide emissions between 1970 and 1980, the Government's objective was to achieve another 30% "by the end of the 1990s", with similar reductions in nitrogen oxides by supporting stricter emission standards from petrol-engined cars and the encouragement of "lean-burn" engine technology. The DOE's stance however was to resist the pressure to install flue gas desulphurisation (FGD) plants at power stations "whilst scientific knowledge is developing and environmental benefit remains uncertain". In support of this position the CEGB evidence was concerned with pricing policies and the effect on both domestic and industrial consumers of the £1.5 billion which an FGD approach would entail.

The committee's decision to mount an investigation was set against the proposition by other European countries that by its stated policy position Britain was not playing its part in fighting the phenomenon (Friends of the Earth, 1984). Nevertheless the select committee's original stance was of neutral enquiry:

> We commenced our enquiry with open minds. We are now convinced, and by our report hope to show, that immediate and hard financial decisions have to be taken as time is running out. Simply to plead for more research into cause and effect is but to procrastinate. Enough is now known to justify the development and application of technology for removing the causes of effects now abundantly apparent. (Rossi, 1985b)

Witnesses confirmed that acid rain is, in the view of an international grouping of environmental activists, one of the major environmental hazards faced by the industrialised world. What it is and what it does are imperfectly understood, and as a consequence there exists a reluctance to take action: a view which the committee and the pressure groups which gave evidence to the enquiry found hard to accept (HC 446 II, 1984).

The committee faced constant difficulty with technical witnesses in the use of the term and used it in their report in the widest possible sense to cover the consequences to water life, the forests, buildings and human health of the chemical changes in the atmosphere produced by emissions from combusted fossil fuels. These emissions may be sulphur dioxide (SO_2), nitrogen oxides (NO_x) or hydro carbons. Their major products are sulphuric and nitric acids, nitrogen dioxide and also ozone.

Prior to the committee's report the British Government, in virtually every parliamentary answer to questions seeking controls, and in response to demands that it should join the '30% club' (that is, countries committed by a protocol to a 30% reduction in their SO_2 emissions between 1980 and 1993), have stood upon the fact that the United Kingdom's emissions of SO_2 have fallen 37% since 1970, considerably closing the gap between the UK and other countries. However, in 1970 the country was and still is to date, the largest producer of SO_2 in Western Europe (Department of the Environment, 1984a).

The committee established during its enquiry that the CEGB, despite its being the major burner of fossil fuels in this country, had made virtually no reduction in its SO_2 emissions. By following a 'tall stacks' policy the CEGB has lessened the acid deposition falling near to power stations but has caused it to be transported over long distances, thus, the committee assumed, increasing the amount of depositions falling in rural areas and even in areas as remote as Scandinavia. Many such areas were shown in evidence, to have been more ecologically sensitive where persistent levels of acid rain can have the worst effects (Central Electricity Generating Board, 1984).

Expert witnesses told members that Britain is the principal foreign depositer of SO_2 in Scandinavia. By 1990 the biggest single polluter of Swedish forests and lakes - even if we join the 30% club - will be the United Kingdom. We already deposit 50% more in Norway than any other country does. It remains the case that in Western Europe only West Germany exports more SO_2 which is deposited in other countries than the United Kingdom (Warren Spring, 1984).

In its report to parliament the thrust of the committee's argument was that by implementing the EC draft directive (Com [83]704) to reduce SO_2 emissions by 60% between 1980 and 1995, the Government now has an opportunity to reverse this state of affairs, and take as positive a step as it did on reducing lead in petrol.

The select committee investigation led to the conclusion that NO_x emissions are largely from the CEGB (55%) and motor cars are major emitters of both NO_x and hydro carbons. Their conclusion was that no significant steps have been taken to control

NO_x and no reductions of significance in NO_x emission have been recorded in the United Kingdom. The EC draft directive requires a reduction in these emissions of 40% by 1995. The committee enquiry covered 10 full days of evidence from experts and representatives of major energy producers, industrial interests and both official and unofficial organisations concerned with the protection of the environment. The minister of state at the DOE was also summoned to the committee. In addition there were detailed memoranda submitted by all those giving evidence and a further 85 pieces of separate written evidence from individuals, experts, companies, professional institutions and international organisations with an interest in the topic. These ranged from the British Lichen Society and the Japanese Ambassador on the one hand to the DTI and the Commission of the European Communities (CEC) on the other.

The committee found among witnesses a deep seated lack of understanding of the complex chemical processes by which the products of fossil fuel emissions cause damage and also a relative lack of public awareness of the problem. By contrast in West Germany there is widespread concern over forest damage, and in Scandinavia over the extensive scale fish-kills in rivers and lakes. It emerged from the enquiry that environments similar to those affected in Scandinavia exist in parts of the United Kingdom but so far only very limited damage has been observed. A dominant feature of the debate before the committee was the demand by some interests in the UK for the proof of the existence of a complete causal chain between emitted pollutant, their derivatives and the observed damage caused. This lack of proof was used by the minister and the CEGB as the best reason not for undertaking action but, rather, for instituting further research - a line of argument with which the committee was reluctant to concur (Forestry Commission, 1984).

Other scientists independent of any manufacturing or industrial interests were convinced that scientific work had advanced far enough for decisions to be taken. They told the committee that like the issue of lead in petrol it had become a matter "of public political will; something will have to be done". The same witnesses told members that there is sufficient evidence on which action should be taken - and various forms of action. These views were endorsed by scientists from abroad and in particular by both Swedish and German government scientists involved in the problems in those countries.

In the course of the enquiry members visited West Germany, Sweden, Norway, Scotland and the Lake District as well as the Central Electricity Research Laboratory at Leatherhead. Discussions encompassed ministers, civil servants, scientists, farmers and those with first hand evidence of acid rain damage. The committee was advised by scientists from the University of Leeds and Imperial College London.

The report deals first with the environmental impact of acid rain and examines in sequence, damage caused to buildings, to lakes, rivers and freshwater life, to trees and plants and damage to materials. Other evidence concerns visibility degradation and the threats to health of acid rain pollution. The investigation then turned to an examination of the polluters and those who suffered from them, with evidence by industrialists and engineers on the scope for emission controls and the costs of the technology required to impose them.

The report arrives at a series of conclusions on each of these aspects of acid rain pollution. First, that it is beyond doubt that acid rain, due mainly to SO_2 emissions, is damaging British buildings and "slowly but surely dissolving our historic heritage". Second, and despite complex natural and chemical interaction in regard to fish and freshwater life that a substantial reduction in SO_2 and NO_x emissions is needed to safeguard the diversity and richness of freshwater life in this country. Evidence from witnesses suggested that mosses and lichens were susceptible to acid deposition and the committee concluded too that there was sufficient evidence that crops and other plant species were damaged enough to cause considerable concern. They recommended that a reduction in SO_2 and NO_x emissions would achieve environmental and ecological benefits. Members arrived at similar conclusions in regard to the corrosion of metals and the degradation of visibility, leading them to urge further research in these areas (Rossi, 1985b).

In regard to human health and despite evidence of increased mercury levels in fish, threats to water supplies and a suggestion of damage to respiratory functions, the enquiry concludes that there was an almost total absence of research which members deprecated. They sought a commitment from the Government that research would be commissioned and would take into account evidence from Swedish, German and US sources with a view to establishing whether risks exist to human health in this country.

Government witnesses did not disagree that the UK is the largest single emitter of SO_2 in the whole of Europe with the exception of the Soviet Union, despite the fact that UK figures have reduced by 37% between 1979 and 1984. Projections by the Department of Energy suggested that in the decade 1980-1990 this country's emissions would fall by less than 5% whilst Germany's would fall by 60% and many other West European countries by 30%. Indeed, the Department of Energy estimated that it was possible, with industrial growth, that emissions might actually rise (Department of the Environment, 1984a).

Eighty per cent of the sulphur deposited in this country is from internal emissions and 28% of our emissions end up in other countries, principally Scandinavia. In quantity terms the UK is second only to West Germany in the amount of sulphur it deposits in other countries. A similar picture emerged for NO_x which, according to the Warren Spring Laboratory (1984) in its evidence to the committee, contributes one-third of acid rain falling in Scandinavia. The Department of Energy's projection was that NO_x emissions in the UK would rise by 10% by the year 2010.

Whilst most of the committee's eventual 21 recommendations to Government concerned the need for further research, the setting up of monitoring arrangements and a commitment to improving existing technology, there were four major recommendations urging that the UK join the '30% club' immediately and that the CEGB should be required to reduce its SO_2 emissions accordingly, with the aim of attaining a 60% reduction by 1995. It urged cooperative work within the EC to agree overall levels of reduction and the development of British technology and research through grants towards development costs.

Evidence during the enquiry both from the minister of state and his scientists indicated that these major recommendations would cost over £1.5 billion for power stations alone. For modifying ten existing major power stations at £150 million each and £35 million of annual operating costs respectively, the Government's estimate was that this would require some 5% addition to domestic electricity bills and incur significant further public expenditure.

The Government's commitment to achieving further reductions was over a longer time scale and did not include a willingness to commit this scale of expenditure on the basis that there was no conclusive evidence that the measures envisaged would solve the problem or indeed, whether ongoing research would provide better solutions.

To this extent the recommendations were rejected:

It is therefore not yet possible to judge whether or when low NO_x burners could become the best practical means of control, and in consequence it would not be sensible to set targets or timetables for emission reductions from existing plants, or emission limits on new plants. There can be no question of the Government assisting industry to convert existing plants; this would be contrary to the 'polluter pays' principle which must apply to NO_x as it does to other emissions. ... Against this background the Government intends to achieve further reductions in national nitrogen oxide emissions from motor vehicles, aiming again at a reduction of 30% of the 1980 levels by the end of the 1990s. (Cmnd 9397, 1984)

The Government also declined to join the '30% club', arguing that the future pattern of industrial structure and energy use is not easy to predict, making it difficult in turn to estimate what further effort and investment might be required in order to be certain of achieving the targets set by the '30% club'. Its response also suggested that there were good prospects for new and better combustion technologies which would lead to reductions in SO_2 emissions being developed as a consequence of research now in hand or foreseen. Two weeks before his appearance before the Environment Committee enquiry on acid rain, the minister, William Waldegrave, had headed the UK delegation to the Munich International Conference on Air Pollution and on 27th June addressed the concluding session. He summed up the British Government's position vis-a-vis its continental neighbours:

And in Britain's case, we have difficulty with only one thing: immediate adoption on top of the nearly 20% reduction made since 1980 in SO_2 emmissions of a binding commitment to a 30% drop by 1993. But we are saying 'yes' to further substantial SO_2 reductions in a reasonable timescale; 'yes' to parallel NO_x reductions; 'yes' to a European-wide onslaught on pollutants from motor-car exhausts; 'yes' to further strengthening of scientific work and monitoring within the ECE Convention, and in other contexts; and above all 'yes' to an international agreement itself.

But if the Government was exhibiting only marginal objection to international aims, the CEGB was considerably more sceptical about EC targets. It told the committee, concerning the draft directive COM (83) 704 that "costs are underestimated by a factor of five, benefits by a substantial amount ... mainly due to a misunderstanding of the causes of alleged damage. Claims that the Directive will be cost-effective are manifestly unsound" (Central Electricity Generating Board, 1984).

In these circumstances neither Government or CEGB were inclined to commit the country to expensive emission controls, especially as there is uncertainty about the environmental benefits to be achieved in this country and in continental Europe. Its formal response to the committee set the bounds of Government cooperation: "the Government intends to achieve further reductions in national S02 emissions, aiming at a reduction of 30% from 1980 levels by the end of the 1990s" (Cmnd 9397, 1984).

The analysis of inputs (see Table 5) to this enquiry shows a preponderance of highly technical data from a range of scientists and academic research bodies. Even the self-interest groups and industrial witnesses produced essentially scientific evidence of a high order. It is the more remarkable that the relatively small volume of evidence from environmental pressure groups, although equally scientifically-based, scored so strongly in terms of shaping the committee's eventual recommendations.

In terms of the weight of argument presented to the committee, the enquiry represented something of a battlefield, with powerful interests such as the Motor Manufacturers Association and the CBI seeking to defend the interests of their members, against pressure groups like Friends of the Earth and the British Lichen Society, whose well-researched argument was supported both by the voice of Scandinavian and West German ecologists and the more neutral factual material presented by a large group of independent and disinterested research institutes and expert witnesses. Major polluters like the CEGB and the National Coal Board (NCB) were mainly concerned to buy time for further research and to budget for incremental expenditure only when all alternative solutions had been examined. Officially sponsored agencies, for example the NCC and those responsible for the fabric of cathedrals, gave dramatic evidence of the need for urgent action to prevent further erosion of historic heritage and environments.

Table 5: Analysis of inputs and citations in the select committee report on acid rain (HC 446, Session 1983/84)

	Ministers/ government departments	Quangos/ official agencies	Local authorities	Self-interest groups	Pressure groups	Independent experts
Witnesses examined	8	3	0	15	3	9
Supporting memoranda	1	0	0	3	1	2
Technical appendices	1	1	0	4	1	3
Other written memoranda/ unpublished evidence	8	20	2	16	9	30
Totals	18	24	2	38	14	44
Citations count	38	86	0	47	12	46
Total inputs	56	110	2	85	26	90
	15.0%	30.0%	0.5%	23.0%	7.0%	24.5%

Figure 7: Matrix assessment - acid rain

Committee: Environment		Topic: Acid rain	
Committee mode: Challenge and monitor objectives	**Policy process intervention:** Evaluation and review	**Issue type:** Technical/scientific	

Input score and citations					
Ministers and government departments	Quangos and official agencies	Local authorities	Self-interest groups	Pressure groups	Independent experts
56	110	2	85	26	90

Government responses to recommendations			
Positive acceptance and action	General agreement	Acceptance for consideration	Neutral comment	Rejection
4	8	3	2	5

In seeking to isolate the key issues for the analysis of effectiveness of the committee (Figure 7), it can be agreed that the topic was essentially of a scientific/technical nature, with most of the argument conducted in those terms, exposing, in the outcome, wide differences of interpretation of evidence, large gaps in understanding and lack of adequate research data from which to extrapolate. The committee is critical of several Government agencies in this regard (HC 446-I, 1984, p xvii).

That the outcome in the Government's response (Cmnd 9397, 1984) was their concurrence with fifteen recommendations and a rejection of only five, masks a rather more substantial resistance to back-bench opinion. In the five recommendations which are rejected, the committee go to the heart of the policy issue which the minister posed to the Munich conference above.

It is in the five rejected recommendations that the major anti-pollution proposals are contained, with demands for the CEGB to undertake radical prevention measures; for the Government to join the commitment of its neighbours in the '30% club' targets; and for industry to have imposed upon it greater anti-pollution measures. The 15 positive responses, in comparison, call for rather less commitment, expenditure or action. Whether or not stung by the criticisms of other nations, the committee's investigation was undertaken in a mode of challenge to current policy stances and the commercial criteria of the energy industries and the CEGB. The committee explicitly set out to monitor current performance and to challenge policy objectives. It collaborated with the experts from countries said to receive most of the polluting emissions 'exported' from the UK and succeeded in at least exposing the differences between what Britain proposes and our neighbours demand by way of combatting the export of industrial acid rain.

The internal debate on these issues had ensured that the Government and its advisers were at the point in their own policy development, of analysing options, evaluating of current targets and reviewing objectives; whether the Environment Committee report, seeking to enter the policy cycle in these areas, was either welcome or effective is a matter that is examined in more depth later in this study.

Case study III: the wealth of waste

Most issues of environmental policy may be fought out between the interests of development and conservation; the needs of technological advance being balanced against the undesirable externalities of pollution or waste of natural resources or danger to health. Advances in environmental policies are often in fact trade-offs premised upon the conception of conflict between economy and environment in which amenity and health are balanced against the economic and technical needs of the polluters (Blowers, 1987).

There is, nevertheless, in the issue of waste reclamation and recycling, a rare coalescence of view between the environmentalist lobby and industrial interests. There are economic benefits, greater profit and very real environmental advantages to be identified in a number of industrial contexts in a planned and comprehensive policy of waste reclamation. When the Trade and Industry Select Committee decided to investigate the whole field of reclamation and recycling, the unanimity of view was marked; only the Government did not have a point of view.

The committee enquiry was prompted by the revelation, in EC statistics, that the UK was low in the league tables of recycling of glass and plastic, rubber, paper and board. Only the scrap metal industry in Britain has a substantial record of recycling of waste (HC 640, 1984). The committee's first discovery was that the Government did not have a policy and in the minister's words, it had "not thought it appropriate to develop a national policy for the sector as a whole" (HC 640, 1984).

In a memorandum to the committee from both the DTI and the DOE, the Government said:

> The Government fully recognise the importance of reclamation and recycling and welcome the cooperation between industry, central and local government and other bodies with interests in the area. It looks to industry, in its own enlightened self-interest to undertake reclamation/recycling where it makes commercial sense to do so. It does not regard such activities as an end in themselves and consequently has not thought it appropriate to develop a national policy for the sector as a whole. (HC 640, 1984)

On the other hand, there was a broad consensus both in the committee and in those giving evidence that more recycling in the UK is desirable on purely narrow commercial grounds, even without taking into consideration the obvious environmental advantages. The committee's report pointed out that recycling leads to a more efficient use of raw material resources and considerable energy savings. A greater reliance on recycled materials reduces the need for virgin raw materials, which in the UK often have to be imported. In addition the recycling of waste (and the production of heat and power through incineration) both reduces the costs of waste disposal and provides income which can be offset against disposal costs. The select committee's report found that despite these powerful economic arguments, the UK failed to produce a well-developed recycling industry. In a few sectors the industry is highly sophisticated, however, it is for the most part very fragmented, having to deal with materials of varying quality and to operate in a fluctuating secondary market.

Evidence sought from sectors where recycling is well organised gives an indication of the scale of economic benefits involved; witnesses demonstrated that the ferrous scrap industry is well established and that some 63% of iron and steel production in 1982 was derived from scrap and waste, approximately half of this coming from the ferrous scrap industry (HC 640, 1984). In the case of certain non-ferrous metals the benefits of recycling are even more marked. Recycling aluminium for instance saves 90% of the energy required to produce aluminium from bauxite.

In the glass industry despite a 'bottle bank' scheme introduced by the Glass Manufacturers Federation, and despite there being nearly 2,000 bottle bank sites collecting 100,000 tons per year, the scheme has not been the success anticipated and the committee found that only 8% of glass consumption was returned in this way. Great Britain was at the bottom of the European league table for glass recycling (HC 640, 1984).

In the case of the waste paper industry the committee found that over 60% of UK use of paper and board is imported and that the waste paper industry itself is doing better in export markets than at home! (HC 640, 1984).

Similarly in the textile field the amount of reclamation in the UK was found to be small-scale and fragmented. With the decline of the home textile industry much of the waste is exported, particularly to Italy. The industry is also hampered by shortages of supply with large quantities of household waste and textiles finding their way into domestic refuse dumps. The committee found that the collection policies of local authorities had a marked effect in this sector.

Other witnesses discussed the inadequacies of plastics recycling and the greater scope for incineration and waste-derived fuel. The potential role for local authorities as both collection and disposal agencies was highlighted by reports from the Greater London Council (GLC) and Leeds City Council where policies in these areas are advanced. The possibilities for improving the performance and the organisation of local government reclamation activity was underlined in the committee's report (HC 640, 1984). The lack of clarity about responsibilities at local level was mirrored by the government departments which gave evidence. This prompted the committee to regret the lack of an overall coordinating role being taken by central government and to criticise the apparent unwillingness of Government to take the lead in promoting recycling schemes where they were economically viable.

The unfortunate ambiguity in Government policy is demonstrated by its inability to decide which department - Environment or Trade and Industry - is the 'lead' department in this area. Officials from the DTI gave evidence that there "is no lead department" but when the minister gave evidence he clearly confirmed that his department was indeed taking the lead. This was then flatly contradicted by William Waldegrave, under secretary of state for the DOE who, in a letter to the committee, said that there was no nominated lead department for recycling as such, but that the DOE is giving the lead for waste management generally. But even whilst affirming his role the minister was unable to state that a specific minister existed with authority across departments and with overall responsibility for recycling policy. The committee highlighted this confusion strongly in its subsequent recommendations (HC 640, 1984).

Another confusion quickly arose. Government ministers expressed the hope that industry would itself take the lead and that the recently formed UK Reclamation Council would fulfill some of the roles sought by the committee. In contrast, the Reclamation Council said in evidence that its major objectives included effective representation of the needs of the industry to central government and a demand that Government itself should stimulate interest in the value of reclamation and recycling. As the committee's report commented, far from doing central government's job for it, the UK Reclamation Council would seem to be yet another organisation which will urge Government to do more.

In the outcome, therefore, the select committee's report was at pains to join with critics from local government and industry in demanding that Government policy should give strong leadership on a national scale: "we are surprised that the Government fails to appreciate either the significance of its own role, or the need for a national policy". The report then went on to outline a policy which it proposed should be adopted by the Government together with ten clear recommendations for implementation.

The report takes a normative tone indicating that the principal actions required of central government in this area are threefold: first, to provide a lead and an overall coordinating role in the promotion and development of recycling; second, to provide incentives to local authorities to investigate the viability of and to set up recycling schemes where appropriate; and third, to stimulate industry to engage in a higher level of recycling.

In all, the committee's report published in October 1984 contained ten specific recommendations including the proposal that one minister should be given overall responsibility across departments for this area of policy, and be empowered to take decisions involving economic, environmental and energy issues. It was proposed that the Government should provide more financial support to the UK Reclamation Council to allow it to promote and publicise recycling schemes together with capital grants to the appropriate tier of local authority for the setting up of specific recycling ventures.

The committee recommended the GLC schemes to other waste disposal authorities and sought government support to extend the arrangement whereby financial rebates are paid to collection authorities for glass recycled through bottle bank schemes. The report also sought the implementation of sections of the Control of Pollution Act 1974 not previously activated, which would give local authorities more power and the ability to spend more and levy charges for the collection of trade waste.

The Government was pressed to give greater incentives to industry for recycling activities and to promote new industrial design schemes in this area. More resources and an enhancement of the existing government research programme at Warren Spring Laboratory were recommended. Members also suggested the use of taxation policy to encourage greater use of recycled material and sought a greater emphasis on public purchasing policy being directed towards encouraging the use of recycled materials whenever economically sensible (HC 640, 1984).

This enquiry is an example of select committee activity exposing an absence of policy, a lack of liaison or cooperation between departments, and a surprising confusion of roles between one minister and another. In economic terms it was able to elicit that if (in 1982) an active policy of waste recycling had been operated, an estimated £750 million of materials could have been re-used (excluding rubber and textiles) by the end of that year. Further, that of the £1.8 billions actually recycled in that year, £1.2 billion was produced by the already efficient ferrous scrap industry (HC 640, 1984).

In policy terms, the select committee also exposed the weakness of the local authority structure which places waste collection duties with the lower tier (district councils and London boroughs) and waste disposal duties with county councils. Thus the authority which incurs the cost of collection does not receive any benefit from introducing recycling schemes. This anomaly led the committee to support the GLC scheme of giving grants to boroughs willing to run glass recycling schemes, and to urge the DOE to take a positive lead in encouraging local authorities in waste reclamation activity. Policy weakness was thus exposed at national, county and district level.

Six months after publication of the select committee recommendations, the Government reply accepted that the report had stimulated a reappraisal of policies and practices; it confirmed that the Government is in favour of recycling where this makes economic sense, and agreed that this assessment should be influenced by the impact on environmental policy and that a long view of what is economic and commercially viable should be taken (HC 321, 1985).

Of the ten specific recommendations of the select committee, the Government responded positively to four and negatively to five (see Figure 8, p 113). The suggestion that there should be a minister given overall responsibility across departments for recycling policy was not agreed. The Government did accept, however, the need for proper coordination and direction of policy and appointed a parliamentary under secretary in the DTI with special coordinating responsibility for waste recycling issues. Although the under secretary was not given decision-making powers in other ministries he was made responsible for identifying inconsistencies or omissions in the policy and for handling parliamentary debates and questions on recycling matters.

The Government agreed to discuss with the UK Reclamation Council the possibility of further financial support for promoting new schemes. They agreed to encourage disposal authorities to initiate schemes such as those that the GLC had introduced, but declined to make further financial resources available. Discussion on the activation of sections 12 to 14 of the Control of Pollution Act 1974 was opened and the Government accepted that it should encourage design promotion schemes in this field and work with industry in supporting further research projects. It also agreed to give encouragement to all public authorities in purchasing policies to make greater use of recycled materials.

The negative aspects of the Government's response were largely to do with finance. The suggestion that further grant aid be given to local authorities was rejected as was the idea of further cash incentives to industry to encourage more recycling schemes. The select committee's suggestion that taxation policy should be used to encourage recycling activity was not accepted.

Both the select committee and the major organisations which gave evidence to it subsequently expressed some disappointment at the 'defensive stance' of the Government's reply although welcoming the serious consideration which the recommendations received and the positive responses which were made. Criticism from the committee of the Government response concerned what its chair called the lack of will to support local authority waste recycling projects, and argued that quite apart from the economic advantages of such a policy, there would be considerable environmental gain from an enhanced scale of activity both by Government and industry.

This point raises, for the policy analysis researcher, the need to examine the mechanisms available for policy making in areas which fall between two or more departments and which may involve conflicting interests or contradictory objectives; in other words, the ability of Government to act 'corporately'. Is it possible to identify a role for all-party select committees?

The absence of a specifically green lobby in this select committee enquiry does suggest that the pressure groups which campaign on environmental issues were not alert to a fundamental question. The environment argument for waste reclamation was subordinate and was left to local authority witnesses and to individual members of the select committee, but the thrust of the debate was economic; it was 'the wealth of waste' retrieval which was at issue and not the quality of the environment. The unspoken implication is that if recycling and reclamation were not economically valuable, it would not be a policy issue. These questions will be taken up later in this study.

A quantitative analysis of the inputs to this investigation (see Table 6) has differentiated the sources of evidence, witnesses and supporting documents into six main categories; the citation of such evidence in the committee's final report is also analysed on the same basis. It suggests that the recommendations were shaped or influenced largely by the evidence of the local authorities and trade groups which gave evidence, and the mode of the committee had been predominantly one of attempting 'to set the agenda', to challenge the ministerial view that it had not been thought appropriate to establish a direct Government policy on reclamation, and to advocate policy initiation (see matrix analysis at Figure 8).

In terms of the policy process model applied here, the committee's intervention has to be seen at the point of issue search and definition. It is significant that although ministers of state and departmental officials had contributed over 20% of the inputs to the investigation their influence on the output of recommendations appears minimal. The essentially economic terms in which the waste reclamation issue was approached with the environmental aspects taking second place, is perhaps due to the fact that the Trade and Industry Select Committee and not the Environment Select Committee undertook the investigation (see Table 3, p 80).

This may be why the analysis is shown to support the high degree of coincidence between the number of recommendations in the final report supported by the inputs from those self-interest groups and local authorities. Figure 8 demonstrates that over 70% of the input score from these sources produces 90% supporting recommendations. Ministers and their departmental officers were responsible for over 20% of input but found an echo in only 10% of recommendations (outcomes). The relatively minor input from the environmental pressure groups to this investigation has, however, still shown to have influenced four out of the ten recommendations.

Table 6: Analysis of inputs and citations in the select committee report of the wealth of waste (HC 640, Session 1984/85)

	Ministers/ government departments	Quangos/ official agencies	Local authorities	Self-interest groups	Pressure groups	Independent experts
Witnesses examined	9	0	5	20	0	1
Supporting memoranda	3	0	2	6	0	0
Technical appendices	3	0	0	9	2	1
Other written memoranda and unpublished evidence	1	5	0	12	3	0
Totals	16	5	7	47	5	2
Citations count	31	0	19	28	7	3
Total inputs	47	5	26	75	12	5
	27.5%	3.0%	15.5%	44.0%	7.0%	3.0%

Figure 8: Matrix assessment - the wealth of waste

Committee: Trade and Industry			Topic: Waste reclamation and recycling	
Committee mode:		**Policy process intervention:**	**Issue type:**	
Agenda-setting/advocate/challenge		Issue definition	Economic	
Input score and citations				
Ministers and government departments	Quangos and official agencies	Local authorities	Self-interest groups	Pressure groups	Independent experts
47	5	26	75	12	5
Government responses to recommendations				
Positive acceptance and action	General agreement	Acceptance for consideration	Neutral comment	Rejection
0	2	2	1	5

eight

ANALYSIS OF THE CASE STUDIES

Introduction

In this chapter, having examined not only the three select committee reports utilised as case studies in Chapter 7 but also applied the same analytical techniques to seven other reports produced during the parliament of 1983-87 in the field of environmental concerns, an assessment of the influence which committee reports and investigations have had on the Government, on policy and on the wider policy community is needed.

In the next part of this study an attempt is made to bring together a quantification of inputs to the ten reports analysed and to test whether either the sources of evidence or any of the three factors identified in Chapters 4 and 5 show markedly varied results, one from another, or in combination.

Table 7 shows, taking all the reports, that of the 248 separate recommendations made by MPs, 145.5 were accepted in some degree. This represents 58.5% of the total. Whilst only 36 (14.5%) were taken up for immediate and positive action, the impact of the others in the longer term, or in influencing approaches or attitudes of administrators or the wider policy community is of some significance and is discussed below in the context of evidence supplied by specialist advisers and other key actors.

Those recommendations accepted for consideration or as the subject of further research have contributed to the 'delayed drop' effect, also discussed below. The outright rejection of committee proposals in Government replies, amounts to 67 (27%) of the total.

Table 7:   Government responses to select committee reports:
environmental issues 1983-87 by type of response

	Positive acceptance and action	General agreement	Acceptance for consideration
Number	36	71	38.5
% of total	14.5	29	15.5

	Neutral comment	Rejection	Total
Number	35.5	67	248
% of total	14.0	27	100

In numerical terms this is a markedly better result than that by committees in the parliament of 1979-83 as assessed by Drewry (1985) in the first study of the new select committee system, although somewhat different methods and definitions were used, and the committee system was not introduced until six months after parliament began sitting.

Drewry and his team admit that they made no serious attempt to evaluate the outcome of recommendations in this way (Drewry, 1985, p 344). Within the totals in Table 7 there are some wide variations. Table 8 provides the breakdown of acceptance and rejection of each report and it will be seen that acceptances vary between 87.5% in the case of the Welsh coastal pollution report to 37% of the committee recommendations in the Historic Buildings and Ancient Monuments investigation. However, apart from the Trade and Industry Select Committee report on waste recycling used as a case study (HC 640, 1984) which had exposed some serious inter-departmental confusions, and half of whose proposals were rejected, all were able to achieve a favourable ratio between acceptance and rejection. In the special circumstances of the gypsy sites review, the 100% acceptance of the committee demand for a review of policy is superficially an important total, but emphasises that willingness to 'review' policy does not always imply changing it. It is in addressing these variations that we need to explore what factors in each enquiry might have affected the outcome.

Table 8:   Analysis of responses to recommendations by select committee report

Report	Positive acceptance and action	General agreement	Acceptance for consideration	Neutral comment	Rejection
Green belt/land for housing HC 275 83/84	7	7.5	4.5	2	5
Acid rain HC 446 83/84	4	8	3	2	5
Acid rain (follow-up) HC 51 85/86	-	-	-	-	-
The wealth of waste HC 640 83/84	0	2	2	1	5
Wildlife and Countryside Act part II HC 6 84/85	2	3	6	4	3
Coastal pollution in wales HC 101 85/86	3	10	1	2	0
Radioactive waste HC 191/HC 211 85/86	8.5	9.5	3.5	6.5	13
Planning: appeals, call-in and major public enquiries HC 181 85/86	2	14.5	2.5	5	12
Pollution of rivers and estuaries HC 183 86/87	5.5	11	9	4	6.5
Historic buildings and ancient monuments HC 146 86/87	3	5.5	7	9	17.5
Caravan Sites Act 1968 HC 414 84/85	1	0	0	0	0

The mode of investigations

Utilising the matrix factors it is evident, for example, that when the committee adopts a 'challenging' mode, as in the enquiries on waste recycling (HC 640, 1984) and radioactive waste (HC 191, 1986) the number of recommendations accepted immediately is lowest. In the case of the acid rain report (HC 446, 1984) which also adopted a challenging mode at some points, the total number of acceptances appear high, but the most important policy recommendations were rejected (see case study). This is not the whole story , as will be evident later, and the longer-term outcome is less dismissive.

This, however, suggests that the latent hostility or fear of select committee investigation among ministers and their advisers referred to by Wass (1984) is likely to lead to political rejection of outrightly critical and challenging reports. However, if they are backed up with well-documented, reputable evidence, especially in the scientific field, the validity of the recommendations may lead to eventual policy change.

When the committee adopts the multiple roles of analyser/ monitor/mediator the scores for accepted recommendations rise substantially. The green belt enquiry (HC 275, 1984), the Wildlife and Countryside Act (HC 6, 1984) and the investigation into pollution of rivers and estuaries (HC 183, 1987) were all investigations by the Environment Committee in these modes. The members were concerned, in the range of witnesses they called and the framing of their reports, to analyse current policy performance and monitor the effectiveness of its application.

In the case of the green belt enquiry there was a role for the committee to mediate between the minister (seeking to restate the balance between green belt protection and the needs of the building industry in a period of growth), and the interests of both environmentalist and developer. The genuine bewilderment within the policy community which emerged in the debate sparked off by the issue of new draft circulars was the main cause of the Environment Committee intervention. The unspoken welcome by ministers of the committee's mediation, hinted at by Rossi, is perhaps reflected in the high level of accepted recommendations (Rossi, 1987).

Part II of the Wildlife and Countryside Act was a recent piece of legislation which rapidly exhibited a 'loophole' in its provisions for protecting sites of special scientific interest and there was a high level of unanimity among witnesses from all the interests involved that it needed to be closed. The evidence submitted to the investigation suggests that the weakness was recognised by the DOE and that following the committee report, parliamentary time was readily facilitated for amending legislation in the form of a private member's bill. The monitoring mode, in which policy is reviewed and short-comings analysed, produces a high level of acceptance in this instance.

Whilst the concept of 'mode' postulated in this hypothesis does not emerge with absolute clarity as a factor of itself and in isolation affecting responses to committee reports, it does appear, as illustrated in Figure 9, that when committees adopt some modes they achieve better results than in others. Those modes which speak of confrontation, or of attempting to establish new agenda or advocacy of a particular cause find less acceptance generally, as well as a higher rate of outright rejection.

Figure 9:   Percentage of recommendations accepted or rejected, by mode of enquiry

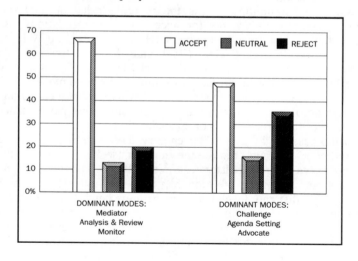

The issue type and mode of committees

It is now necessary to consider whether the mode of a select committee enquiry, combined with the type of issue under investigation, together achieve more positive responses in some combinations than in others.

It will be recalled that three issue types were identified among the ten reports considered. They were typified as:

- administrative;

- technical/scientific;

- economic.

These issue types are defined in detail in Chapter 5. Table 9 sets out in tabular form the mode and type of issue and the point of intervention in the policy life-cycle of each of the enquiries being considered, juxtaposed with the percentage of recommendations accepted and rejected in Government responses. For this exercise, the proposals given a 'neutral' response are left out of the calculation.

It is evident at once that the administrative topics achieve mixed scores. At times it is high, especially when associated with a style of enquiry which is concerned with analysis of problems and review of performance, or monitoring of effectiveness; less well in others. The administrative issues are those in which bureaucratic processes or regulatory rules are under consideration, or, it is argued, where the policy has passed the stage of political analysis and debate in the policy life-cycle and are by their nature, mainly in the realms of administrative implementation. Departmental officials rather than ministers were expected to answer for the efficiency and effectiveness of the policy delivery or practice; or, in the case of the green belt enquiry and the planning enquiry, the implementation by local authorities and other official agencies were in question.

The green belt investigation dwelt principally on the efficiency of the processes of defining and protecting green belt boundaries and the local authority procedures for dealing with planning applications for development. The 73% of recommendations accepted were largely concerned with modifying these procedures.

Table 9: Analysis of recommendations accepted or rejected, by mode, issue type and intervention

Committee report	Dominant mode/s	Issue type	Point of intervention	Recommendations (%)	
				Accept	Reject
Green belt/land for housing	Mediator/analyser	Administrative	Implementation monitor/control	73.0	19.5
Acid rain	Challenge/monitor	Technical/scientific	Evaluation/review	68.0	22.5
Wealth of waste	Agenda setting/advocate/challenge	Economic	Issue definition	40.0	50.0
Wildlife and Countryside Act part II	Analysis/review/monitor	Administrative	Implementation/control	61.0	16.5
Coastal pollution in Wales	Analysis/monitor	Technical/scientific	Evaluation/review	87.5	0
Radioactive Waste	Challenge/monitor	Technical/scientific	Option analysis	45.0	31.5
Planning: appeals, call-in and major public enquiries	Analysis/monitor	Administrative	Evaluation/review	52.5	33.5
Pollution of rivers and estuaries	Analysis/review	Technical/scientific	Setting objectives/priorities	71.0	18.0
Historic buildings	Mediator/Prioritiser	Administrative	Implementation/control	37.0	41.5
Gypsy sites	Analysis/review/monitor	Administrative	Evaluation/review	100.0	0

Note: recommendations receiving a 'neutral' response have been omitted from this calculation.

Similarly, the report on Part II of the Wildlife and Countryside Act, 61% of whose recommendations were accepted, was concerned to evaluate and improve the procedures for authorities and agencies such as the NCC in administering the Act. The same context obtains in the report 'Planning: appeals, call-in and major public enquiries' (HC 181, 1986).

The Environment Committee's comment on the slow progress in implementing the 1968 Caravan Sites Act (HC 414, 1985) and their demand for a review of performance of the mandatory duties placed upon local authorities to create gypsy sites, produced a quick, favourable response from the DOE which commissioned an independent review.

The remaining enquiry of an administrative topic into the management of historic buildings and ancient monuments, was less acceptable, however, to the DOE; only 37% of its recommendations were adopted. It is perhaps the case that the complex relationships between the DOE, English Heritage, and a range of other official, voluntary and private bodies make immediate response less simple, but it is not without significance that the minister, in response to the committee, commented:

[The Report] is a valuable starting point and a rich quarry of ideas and data for the refinement and the development of policy towards the heritage ... and is likely to remain valid for this purpose for a considerable time to come. (HC 268, 1988)

In all, the total number of recommendations in enquiries related to administrative issue types was 123 of which 53.5% were accepted, whilst 30% were rejected (see Figure 10).

The one investigation in which the issues were predominantly economic was that relating to waste recycling (HC 640, 1984). Uniquely, of the reports under review, it was undertaken by the Trade and Industry Select Committee and was demonstrably in a mode of attempting to 'set the agenda' or to bring new policy into the Government's programme. The argument, both of the committee and many of its witnesses was conducted in terms of the economic advantages to be gained from a policy of encouraging more recycling of industrial waste (see case study). The environmental arguments were understated, and the departmental view that recycling was essentially a matter for commercial judgement, was challenged by the report. The combination of a challenging or agenda-setting mode and 'economic' issue type appears to get the largest percentage of active rejection of its recommendations (Figure 10). However, on the basis of one example, the assessment must be tentative.

Figure 10: Percentage of recommendations accepted or rejected by issue type

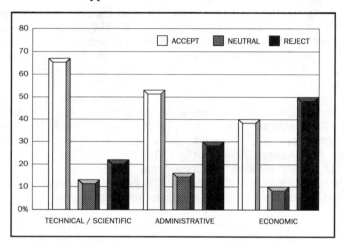

The four major enquiries which were of a technical/scientific issue type were perhaps also topics with the highest political profile, touching upon environmental concerns rapidly emerging in the public consciousness as important elements in the green agenda, not only in the UK, but in the international debate about ecological conservation.

The production of acid rain from fossil fuel power stations and its effect upon forests and lakes; the pollution of beaches and of waterways from illegal dumping at sea; uncontrolled or badly maintained sewage plant and agricultural pesticides; and the apparently insoluble problems of how, safely, to store radioactive wastes, have become topics at the very top of the international political agenda, since these reports were published.

In the parliament of 1983-87 they were not, perhaps, quite so sensitive or immediate. Nevertheless the policy community within which much of the select committee debate took place was alive to the scale of the problems. The larger agencies such as the CEGB and the Nuclear Industry Radioactive Waste Executive (NIREX), and the self-interest groups such as the NFU and the water authorities were meticulous and thorough in the scientific quality of their evidence. Similarly, the range of pressure groups and independent experts who presented papers from eminent scientists or academic sources is impressive. Key actors in the process stress that whatever else was achieved, the reports of the enquiries such as those into radioactive waste and acid rain form a comprehensive 'state-of-the-art' compendium of current scientific knowledge (Patterson, 1988; Porritt, 1988).

The special adviser appointed by the Environment Committee for the radioactive waste investigation is explicit:

> Reports of this kind are part of an educational process for departmental civil servants. They expose inconsistencies and comprise a basic textbook of technical information, bringing together in a concise way, the stated position of all the participants; an invaluable compendium of the present state of knowledge. The Rad-waste report is in fact a position statement in a fast developing technology. (Patterson, 1988)

Figure 10 illustrates that when technical/scientific topics formed the content of an investigation, the level of accepted recommendations is higher than when administrative or economic issue types are chosen. This view is borne out by the fact that out of a total of 115 recommendations in all on technical/scientific issues, 66% were accepted to some degree, whilst 21% were rejected. They are highest when associated with a mode of analysis and review or monitoring performance, as in the coastal pollution enquiry with 87.5%, and the pollution of rivers and estuaries report with 71% (see Table 9, p 120). When the committee is in challenging mode the level of acceptance drops to 68% and 45%, lending support to the view that mode and issue type have a bearing together on the outcome.

Intervention in the policy life-cycle

The third factor, in terms of the hypothesis expounded here, which may have a bearing on select committee influence on Government policies is that of the point of intervention in the life-cycle of policy. In Chapter 4 a model of the policy process derived from Hogwood and Gunn (1984) was constructed, as illustrated in Figure 3 (p 54), and in each of the committee reports examined it was established at which point in the policy life-cycle that particular subject was located. In other words, the question to be asked was: where in the life of this topic or policy is the committee seeking to intervene?

Table 9 (p 120) sets out in tabular form for each of the reports reviewed, not only the mode and issue type, but also the policy cycle intervention point, and this allows us to consider whether, in addition to measuring the fate of committee recommendations by mode and type, the stage in the policy life-cycle at the time of the investigation was significant, or produces any pattern which can be described.

It would appear that, in the reports examined here, there is a higher percentage of committee recommendations accepted in those instances where policy is in the implementation phase, or is being monitored, or is at the stage of evaluation or review of effectiveness. In the earlier phases of the cyclical journey, intervention appears less successful. Figure 11 plots this finding.

Figure 11: Percentage of recommendations approved illustrated at the point of intervention in the policy life-cycle

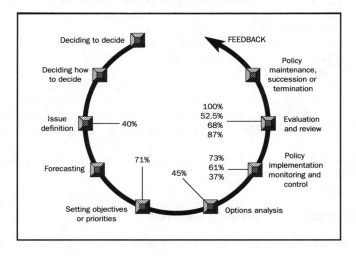

Note: This figure demonstrates, taking the percentage of committee recommendations from each report accepted by Government (set out in Table 9), the point in the policy life-cycle at which the impact occurred.

However, since none of the reports reviewed dealt with policies which were at the very early stages of formation or were at the end of their life-cycle, it is not possible from the research undertaken here to say whether they would have been more or less successful.

Indeed, it could be argued that if committees examined policy options in the formative stages of the process, perhaps by deciding to examine all Green Paper proposals and commenting on all White Paper proposals, they might be more effective in influencing ministers and their advisers. It is evident from the committee activities under review that members have tended to be reactive and to take up the issues in the wake of public or other criticism of the effect of policy or failure of policy measures, rather than to take the initiative at the point when policy options are being discussed or issues being defined. This point is underlined by the one report which dealt with policies at the point of setting objectives and priorities, when 71% of the recommendations were approved (see Figure 11).

On the economic topic of waste recycling, in which the Trade and Industry Committee took a challenging mode, and when the Government was itself in the process of defining its policy stance, the outcome in terms of acceptances and rejections of committee recommendations is least favourable to the select committee.

Inputs of evidence

In concluding this part of the analysis we should turn now to the final element in the matrix approach and consider, in the terms of the 'black box' model, whether the inputs from various sources have any bearing upon the outcomes, in terms of the acceptance of reports and recommendations.

For this enumeration, all the inputs to each of the select committee reports under review were totalled, including the number of memoranda, technical appendices, unpublished documents and the witnesses who appeared. To these figures were added the number of occasions in each report when particular witnesses or documents were cited in the formulation of recommendations. Thus a total number of inputs to each enquiry is arrived at, and is then categorised into one of six groups of sources as follows:

- ministers and departments;
- quangos and official agencies;
- local authorities;
- self-interest groups;
- pressure groups;
- independent experts.

Table 10 provides a breakdown of inputs from these six sources for each of the ten reports considered and allows some examination to be undertaken as to whether the volume and source of inputs relates in any way to outcomes and whether there are patterns to be found in relation to the rate of acceptance or rejection of committee recommendations.

Table 10: Sources of inputs to select committee enquiries

Source	Ministers and departments	Quangos and official organisations	Local authorities
Number	737	687	458
% of total	20.2	18.7	12.5

Source	Self-interest groups	Pressure groups	Independent experts	Totals
Number	646	532	605	3,665
% of total	17.6	14.5	16.5	100

First, the breakdown of the total contributions to all ten reports (Table 11) demonstrates a pattern of activity which may give some clues as to the way in which select committee investigations are seen by the world external to parliament, and the value members and committee officials place upon the wider world of policy interest. Whilst ministers and their advisers are still numerically the greatest source of input, they are not so dominant as reported in other earlier studies (see Hill, 1984, p 200).

Table 11: Table of inputs of evidence for each enquiry, by source

Report	Ministers/ government departments	Quangos/ official agencies	Local authorities	Self- interest groups	Pressure groups	Independent experts
Green belt/land for housing HC 275 83/84	50	-	134	43	30	28
Acid rain HC 446 83/84	56	110	2	85	26	90
Acid rain (follow-up) HC 51 85/86	-	-	-	-	-	-
The wealth of waste HC 640 83/84	47	5	26	75	12	5
Wildlife and Countryside Act Part II HC 6 84/85	14	85	37	58	149	21
Coastal pollution in Wales HC 101 85/86	18	49	21	2	13	90
Radioactive waste HC 191 HC 211 85/86	165	183	123	133	48	140
Planning: appeals, call-in and major public enquiries HC 181 85/86	167	19	40	123	77	115
Pollution of rivers and estuaries HC 183 85/86	128	145	7	49	37	67
Historic buildings and ancient monuments HC 146 86/87	88	91	41	76	113	44
Caravan Sites Act 1968 HC 414 84/85	4		27	2	27	5
Total inputs	737	687	458	646	532	605
% of total	20.2	18.7	12.5	17.6	14.5	16.5

It is, as we saw earlier, essentially the chair and clerk who are the 'gatekeepers' in the flow of evidence and submissions to the investigative process (Gren, 1987; Rossi, 1987). It is they who invite contributions from the policy community and subsequently draw on those contributions in writing their reports and recommendations. In this sense the inputs are a factor of the investigation process itself. Viewed in this way certain trends emerge which are discussed below. It is also evident from a study of the evidence volumes of the reports discussed in this analysis that ministers and departmental officials in the main confined their contributions to giving facts and answering questions as did the official agencies. It was left to the pressure groups and those with a commercial or economic self-interest to make recommendations or press a case for change. Local government too, in the cases in which they were key actors or implementers, were frequently making a collective case or positive recommendations. Most often, the independent expert witnesses were asked to comment or advise, although in some instances they too came forward with positive recommendations.

The local authority role

In terms of the content of the ten reports on environmental issues it is notable that the local authority input is comparatively low (see Tables 10 and 11). Given the role which they have in the operation and regulation of much of the environmental legislation and the fact that they are traditionally the forum for expressing public opinion in local affairs, not least in the defence of local amenity, it is remarkable that their collective input is least.

This relative paucity of local government contribution suggests a degree of marginalisation; another example of the diminution of local authority role and responsibilities reflected across a wide range of policy in the 1980s. Alternatively, local authorities collectively have not perceived that the work of select committees may be an important plank in the central/local policy interchange. The same point is noted by a special adviser to the Environment Committee but is accounted for by what he suggests is the poor quality of evidence and witnesses produced by authorities in many cases: "they tended to waffle" (Grant, 1988).

There is explicit exemplification of this in a later investigation by the Environment Committee into toxic waste disposal (HC 22,

Session 1988/99), in which the role of councils as waste disposal authorities is excoriated in terms rarely seen in select committee reports; epithets ranging from 'scandalous' and 'inadequate' to 'utter nonsense' being used to describe councils' performances.

The one example in which the local government inputs are substantially the greatest is in the green belt/land for housing investigation (HC 275, 1984); in that case, a number of well-researched papers were submitted by county councils, metropolitan and borough authorities and the GLC. Four separate evidence sessions were devoted to examining these witnesses - councillors and officers as well as planning professionals - out of a total of twelve such sessions in all. Table 11 indicates that this amounted to 134 (37%) of 285 inputs in all. A number of recommendations made by these witnesses were reflected in the final report which recorded 63 local authority citations from a total of 147 citation inputs (see Table 4).

Pressure groups and technical topics

Another distinct trend in this analysis indicates that the reports which were of a technical/scientific issue type rely heavily on evidence from the departments, from official agencies or from independent experts rather than from other sources. Whilst this will not, in itself, be surprising and is mirrored by a low level of input from pressure groups (7% in the acid rain investigation, 6.5% in Welsh coastal pollution and 6% in radioactive waste) this low input is not always represented by low citations. This suggests that for some groups of witnesses, quality of input does not equate with quantity, since the environmentalist lobby in these instances was able to influence both the tone and content of recommendations in a way not achieved by local authority witnesses.

To test this proposition some of the large and influential pressure groups who are frequently invited to give evidence on environmental issues, were invited for the purposes of this study, to review the specific recommendations they had made and to evaluate the influence they had, both in the committee's formal recommendations and in the Government's response to them. This exercise covered the reports on pollution of rivers and estuaries (HC 183, Session 1985/86), and planning (HC 181, Session 1985/86). The sample covers a spectrum of groups from the radical 'direct action' internationally organised Greenpeace, to the long-standing traditional rural lobby represented in the Council for the Protection of Rural England (see Table 12).

The participants in this exercise comment upon the difficulty of being certain whether their argument is accepted or not. In the case of the river pollution debate, the 'goal-posts' were moved dramatically half-way through when the Government announced its privatisation plans for the water industry. The issue, therefore, is whether, in the outcome, the anti-pollution measures imposed upon the privatised industry by statute, match the committee's recommendations.

The CPRE argument to the planning investigation stressed the importance of engendering a change of attitude by all participants, and to this extent the very process of giving evidence, publishing a committee report and a Government response, does as much to shift attitudinal stances throughout the planning community, as do specific detailed proposals (Bate, 1989). This compliments the view of the special adviser who records the opinion that the committee report was widely utilised both in practice and in teaching. Table 12 demonstrates that 50% of pressure group recommendations (input) are reflected in the committee report (output); it is less clear that in terms of outcome, (Government action) the same success rate is achieved. CPRE reports that its recommendations to the planning investigation were "progressively diluted" until the Government's response bore little resemblance to CPRE's initial submission (Council for the Protection of Rural England, 1984).

In order to understand the subtlety and complexity of determining this relationship, and the incremental nature of policy change, the micro-level needs to be examined including an example of input, output and outcomes and to note the differing emphasis or transformation which can take place as the system takes in an idea, and ejects it at the other end of the process.

An example of one relatively minor recommendation, made in evidence to the river pollution enquiry by Greenpeace, and its fate is traced in the select committee process is given on p 132.

Table 12: Pressure group recommendations: how they fared

Group	Enquiry	Issue type	Recs made	Recs accepted by committee	Overall response to evidence from: * committee	government
Greenpeace	Pollution of rivers and estuaries	Technical/ scientific	6	5	Significantly	Moderately
Council for the Protection of Rural England	Planning: appeals, call-in and major public enquiries	Administrative	14	7	Significantly	Moderately
Friends of the Earth	Pollution of rivers and estuaries	Technical/ scientific	24	10	Moderately	Moderately

Note: * Respondents were asked to indicate how far their proposals, taken as a whole, were reflected in the
Government's/committee's response, either specifically or by implication

Input output and outcome: an example

Input

Recommendation 4 of Greenpeace memorandum to the Environmental Committee (HC 183 1986/87, p 208)

An urgent need is perceived for an aquatic toxicity database with incorporation of data concerning responses of a wide variety of organisms. Testing procedures should be implemented to take account of differential sensitivities of organisms relative to their life-cycle. Sensitive faunal components should be tested in addition to species of commercial importance.

Output

Recommendations 28 and 29 of the Environment Select Committee report on pollution of rivers and estuaries (HC 183, 1986/87, vol 1)

Provision by chemical companies to their customers of data on the hazardous effects of their products in the environment and in aquatic toxicity levels, as well as inspection of their customers' storage facilities, are worthwhile measures. We recommend that DOE and the Health and Safety Executive together with the Chemical Industries Association (CIA) and CBI should consider whether such schemes should be introduced here. ... There should be a pooled index system, to which water authorities have access, with information on the properties of dangerous chemicals ... in regard to organisms.

Outcomes

1) DOE response to the Environment Committee (HC 543, 1987/88, paras 4.16 to 4.18)
   The provision of adequate data on the hazardous effects of chemicals on the environment is necessarily difficult because of the wide range of possible situations. ...Government is actively participating in discussions at European Community

level on more comprehensive provisions for the classification and labelling of substances dangerous to the water environment. ... The proposal for a pooled index system is an interesting one, but it should be recalled that a number of databases and databanks holding information on the properties of chemicals, including their environmental effects, already exists. The construction and maintenance of a pooled index system, accessible to water authorities ... would be a very large task, and in view of the lack of full information on possible environmental hazards it is not clear [there would be] great advantage over existing systems. However, government departments will keep the issue under close review in the light of developments.

2) The Water Bill, published in February 1989, contains powers for the minister to regulate by order, the water industry to maintain databanks on hazardous chemical pollutants and to carry out research into the effects of aquatic toxicity in rivers and estuarine waters.

3) Government announced its acceptance of a European Community decision which extends the Community information system for the control of marine pollution caused by spillage to cover inland waterways. The system requires national governments to keep an inventory of toxic materials, their effects on marine organisms, and toxicity levels. (Council Decision 16/17 June 1988, European Information Service Bulletin 80, p 13).

This evidence and the illustration of a micro-level example of one small piece of advice, in input/output terms, is illustrative of the contention that there are limitations to a quantitative assessment of citations of evidence, and provides further support for a parallel qualitative examination, which is pursued in the next chapter.

These examples also tend to confirm that pressure group influence was greatest in those cases where policy was at the evaluation and review stage or, in the case of the Wildlife and Countryside Act enquiry, was firmly in the implementation stage. A committee chair confirms this impression:

> We felt pressure groups like Greenpeace and Friends of the Earth were valuable witnesses when they could bring evidence of a practical kind about the successes and failures of policy operating on the ground. ... I think we were less impressed when they were polemical and arguing a more ideological case of their own. (Rossi, 1987)

Despite this view there is evidence that the growth of the select committee phenomenon has produced effects on the role and status of both the self-interest groups and pressure groups themselves, not yet fully reflected in the analytical literature.

In most committee investigations the self-interest groups appear to exert far greater influence than the count of inputs would imply. In only one of the enquiries (the wealth of waste) do their input scores (or the citations made from them) reach the highest comparative level; and that was an economic topic in agenda-setting/advocate mode, which scored least in acceptances. In all the others, the influence is less easy to pinpoint, less specific or obvious than some other strands of influence, which leads to a closer look at the countervailing influences which the fact of select committee access produces in the groups which attempt to utilise them.

Interest group involvement

In a recent study Jordan and Richardson (1989) emphasise the normality of interest group activity, their contribution to the responsiveness of policy making and continuities in the process of interest group accommodation. They assert that pressure group activity is "a normal, indeed commonplace aspect of a developed polity".

Whilst it can be agreed that groups continue to play an important representational role, it is evident that the balance has been tilted under recent Conservative Governments, in favour of the Executive, and the structures under which their consent is mobilised are modified. Select committees are becoming an important part of the mechanisms which mediate group-government relations. Indeed, committees are cementing the process of interest group integration in contemporary Britain. The agenda-setting role of interest groups is maintained, even enhanced, because although it is a committee and its chair which formally choose topics and set committee programmes, it has been shown that the nature of the debate, the emphasis and direction, especially in technical/scientific issue types, is largely determined by the evidence and memoranda of issue-based pressure groups, counterpointed by those self-interest groups and stakeholders, whose inputs we have calculated above.

But Jordan and Richardson discern a new sectorisation of policy making and the development of policy communities which, they argue, may work towards the disaggregation of all policy issues. They point to the disparity between the agenda of the group and Government world and that of parliament and the media as evidence of this segmentation and the complexity of policy making (Jordan and Richardson, 1989). This study of select committee work has shown that the relationship between science and the development of environment policy is one such issue which exemplifies the point and which is examined in a later chapter.

Commentators, such as Marsh (1983), have stressed the differences between 'economic' groups, formed to protect and promote the specific trading interests of their members, and 'ideological' groupings promoting or defending legislative or administrative change on moral, philanthropic or public good grounds.

It is also evident from the literature that there have been a number of changes in what Schmitter (1979) termed patterns of interest group intermediation, during the 1970s. First, the number and range of groups has multiplied. Second, the propensity for such groups to engage in political lobbying has increased, and third, such groups have emphasised contacts with the Executive, rather than with parties and parliament.

In the 1980s, however, the Conservative Government under Mrs Thatcher stressed commitment to less intervention and to cabinet prescription, reducing the potential for formalised direct contacts between interest groups and Government. This has tended to emphasise the need for contact with and the usefulness of relations with select committees.

The causes underlying these changes may have to do with the apparent reduction in quangos, with the widespread deregulation in many areas of social and economic life, and with the breaking down of professional monopoly, all tending to reduce the status of groups which had achieved 'insider' legitimacy in the corporatist environment of the 1960s and 70s.

Commentators such as Marsh (1983) and Richardson and Jordan (1979) note the significant difference in patterns which developed in various policy communities. The kind of corporatist patterns which emerged in the economic/industrial policy areas were not apparent in social policy areas.

The evidence in this study suggests that the pattern in environmental policy development varies depending upon whether any economic interests are involved. This is particularly well illustrated in the case of the waste recycling and planning investigations and in green belt debates where the self-interest groups such as the NFU and the development industry and large trade associations, achieve inputs on a scale consistently larger than those ideological or 'outsider' lobbies are able to do (see Table 11, p 127).

The new component, the presence of the select committee itself, however, considerably complicates the earlier patterns of intermediation, whether they are defined in pluralist or corporatist terms. The select committee process has:

● ensured that the case made by these powerful self-interest groups is exposed to the analysis of the 'outsider' groups such as Friends of the Earth and Greenpeace; this is not so much a process of incorporation as a counterbalancing weight of argument;

● the ambivalent relationship between 'direct action' or radical campaigning groups and authority is mitigated by the authoritative, technically proficient evidence which they bring to the committee's attention;

● in the select committee process, the close relationships between 'insider' groups and nationalised or official agencies such as the CEGB and the electrical appliance industry, is exposed to examination in a way not achieved before;

● the 'outsider' groups take at least one step over the Westminster threshold when they utilise the select committee enquiry to make their case and are by no means relegated to the tradesman's entrance; in other words a degree of legitimation is achieved which may fall short of incorporation but is nonetheless significant.

It has been indicated above that another aspect of the new committees' role is their impact upon those within the policy community; that there are modifications to the way interest groups and pressure groups act themselves. Groups which submit themselves to select committee enquiries are required to justify their sectional aspirations in terms of the public interest, and to formulate their arguments in the knowledge of the published evidence of departments and ministers (Marsh, 1986). In this context Marsh argues for select committees as what he terms "agents of parliament": to be catalysts for broadening the access and participation of interest groups, and to have a formal role in the mobilising of consent.

Summary

From the evidence evinced by this attempt to establish a triangulated relationship of three key factors underlying select committee investigations, certain clear trends or patterns begin to emerge. When committees adopt particular approaches to investigations or have clear implied purposes in mind and are dealing with some types of policy or administrative problems, they consistently fare better than in other modes and subject matter. They appear to fare least well when attempting to modify Government economic objectives.

Whilst it would not be safe to draw any firm or incontrovertible conclusions about those forces which would ensure that select committee enquiries attain influence on Governments or departments of state, some clear strands do emerge, especially in the relationship between the kinds of issues taken up by members and the style in which the investigation is conducted. On the other hand, the arbitrary way in which committees decide to undertake investigations allows no clear, prescriptive judgements about when, in the life-cycle of a policy, intervention will have the greatest effect.

It is, however, possible to conclude that highly complex technical or scientific issues, taken up on the basis of collecting the most advanced knowledge and the broadest spectrum of expert opinion, and in a mode which does not so much challenge as supplement the Government's own state of knowledge, is likely to find acceptance.

Both administrative and scientific subjects do well in terms of acceptance of recommendations when the investigations are undertaken in non-confrontational modes (see Table 9, p 120). Similarly, challenges to underlying economic strategies or to strongly-held ideological stances are the least likely to exert influence. This is not to say that committees cannot successfully oppose and expose Government actions in matters of great public moment or party ideology. There are indeed a number of much-quoted instances since 1979 in which committees have successfully brought issues of a highly embarrassing kind into public scrutiny, achieving a change or clarification of policy or position. The Agriculture Committee, the Defence Committee, the Social Services Committee and the Environment Committee have all made this kind of impact, particularly in more recent history of the select committee system. (For a discussion of these topics see Field, 1988; Hennessy, 1989; Ryle and Richards, 1988.)

As Giddings (1985) has pointed out, it was never the intention of the system that it should have the reversal of policy or change of administrative decision as a major aim. On the contrary it was neither expected, nor did it seek, to impose wholesale changes on Government policy or administration. The process is more subtle; words such as 'influence', 'monitoring' and 'education' crop up most frequently. The most successful reports described here rely more on achieving constructive dialogue, or on widening or informing the debate on complex issues or policy development. The degree of long-term influence on policy change or on priorities is subtly difficult to pin down, although later pages of this book will provide glimpses of that process in action.

The quantitative significance of the analysis of inputs should not, on the evidence here, be overstated or indeed used to draw particular conclusions (see Table 10, p 126). Its value rather is in the patterns of activity which it reveals and the indications it gives of the process; that some evidence appears to have more impact than others. This particular glimpse into the 'sealed box' of the committee system will not allow of simplistic statistical formulae; if the way the committee utilises its material can be discerned from the citations which the report writers make, then it is rather a basis for drawing tentative conclusions and for following, in a reflective way, the insights and trends which emerge. For example, the acid rain enquiry shows that although the committee received only 24 inputs from quangos and official agencies, it cited the material 86 times in formulating its reports. In the investigation into Part II of the Wildlife and Countryside Act, there were only 8 inputs from these bodies but they were referred to 72 times.

Indeed the evidence from ministers and their departments and from official agencies is consistently quoted more often than other kinds of evidence whether in administrative or technical/scientific topics.

To illustrate the point, Table 13 displays the inputs and citations in two groups, distinguishing between technical and administrative reports, and allows us to see more clearly the relationship between inputs and citations of various sources of evidence in the two types of investigation.

These indications of the weight given to particular evidence are not always echoed in the relationship between evidence and recommendations of witnesses on the one hand and the conclusions of the select committees on the other. This validates the suggestion from the pressure groups in the survey conducted above that their influence is greater and more sustained than has so far been acknowledged. The perception of these participant groups, external to the parliamentary system, whether 'insider' or 'outsider' in status, suggests they are finding the select committee a productive and receptive vehicle for the kind of detailed and complex case made in support of both administrative and policy change, especially in the technical and scientific debates which much environmental policy encompasses. The CPRE for example believe it is "an extremely useful forum for us to put across our more visionary ideas in the context of constructive debate. They have been helpful in encouraging us to set down on paper our views and hopes on one issue after another" (Bate, 1989).

If their case is not immediately conceded, either by the committee or by Government, then there is other evidence to suggest that it plays some part in the longer-term processes of policy change and formation. Evidence from MPs active in the committee process examined in the next chapter leads to this conclusion and it is the nature of this phenomenon which needs understanding in order to enrich the matrix approach adopted so far.

What this analytical matrix approach to select committee activity illustrates, together with the numerical evaluation of its inputs, outputs and outcomes, is that whilst 'mode' and 'issue type' are relevant factors in the assessment of a committee's activities, and the point of intervention in the life-cycle of a policy will affect the outcome of an enquiry, other factors too must be understood and may be more instrumental in achieving change.

Table 13: Input to citation ratio: administrative and technical/scientific topics

Source of evidence	Administrative issue types				Technical/scientific issue types			
	Inputs		Citations		Inputs		Citations	
	No	%	No	%	No	%	No	%
Ministers/departments	33	8.0	198	25.5	87	17.0	280	22.0
Quangos/official agencies	14	3.5	90	11.5	98	19.5	389	30.5
Local authorities	117	28.5	94	12.0	50	10.0	103	8.0
Self-interest groups	70	17.0	155	20.0	101	20.0	168	13.5
Pressure groups	115	28.0	141	18.0	63	12.5	56	4.5
Independent experts	63	15.0	101	13.0	107	21.0	270	21.5

Perhaps the key point is that the inquisitorial and reflective nature of the committee process is not well catered for in other parts of the parliamentary process and it therefore tends to have an illuminating or enlightening, rather than a direct problem-solving role.

The collation of evidence and research does not, in these examples, directly produce major policy change, but it changes the nature of the debate, colouring the context and having the kind of gradual impact upon policy makers which may never be attributed back directly to the original work or the committee report which elicited it.

This study argues that this imperceptible contextual shift, affecting departmental advisers, ministers, back benchers and other non-parliamentary actors in the policy communities, adds up to far more than simply the pursuit of 'explanatory dialogues', in which terms one commentator has most recently characterised select committees (Johnson, 1988, p 183). Whilst acknowledging Johnson's case that select committees do not make, or decisively change policy, it is possible to demonstrate a far from marginal impact on the direction and awareness of Government actions in environmental matters and the role of the state in limiting the damage to ecological systems and the global environment of advanced industrial societies such as the UK.

Another factor, not yet picked up by the political analysts, but emerging in the work of the Environment Committee is the cumulative impact of a consistent series of reports, now stretching over three parliaments, on one area of policy. The acid rain report in 1984 (HC 446, 1984) and its follow-up (HC 51, 1986); air pollution (HC 270, 1988); and toxic waste (HC 22, 1989) amount to an impressive body of scientific evidence constant in its argument and the high quality of its case for policy advance.

The Environment Committee chair makes the point succinctly:

From our work on environmental issues over a number of years, we sense a growing concern, as much from within industry as without, for consistent effective and scientifically justified environmental protection against every separate source of danger. We consider that the DOE has failed to provide the leadership and commitment necessary to achieve this. It can only be obtained by a more cohesive system of regulation and we consider the time is ripe for a major new agency, which would integrate the current fragmented system and provide the sustained motivation and direction necessary on environmental issues. (Rossi, 1989a)

The degree to which this long-term attention produces heightened awareness of public opinion, better media understanding and a coherence and uniformity of argument may have, in the longer term, important political consequences.

In the next chapter other elements of this essentially evolutionary process will be examined using the techniques of pluralistic evaluation and starting with the insights of those most central of participants, the committee members themselves.

nine

QUALITATIVE APPROACHES TO ASSESSING COMMITTEE EFFECTIVENESS

Introduction

It has been argued that select committees are emerging as intermediary agencies allowing interests and arguments to be deployed almost at the heart of the parliamentary process. As the Government distances itself from a legislative programme of widespread deregulatory privatising and centralist policy making, which seems at times to bypass the floor of the House of Commons, some parliamentarians view the select committee as one of the few remaining antidotes to prime ministerial dictat (Emery, 1989).

There is a view emerging, illustrated by the comments recorded here from some of the major pressure groups and from participant MPs, that throughout the 1980s as the Executive grew less responsive, even to its own back-bench opinion, parliament became a vital link in the chain of pluralist policy mediation through the committee system. Back benchers gain expertise and use it in other parliamentary arenas, questions to ministers are more incisive and departmental advisers more open to ideas.

So far this study has relied upon numerical evaluation of material to assess the impact of committees on departmental policy and the influences which lead committees to formulate sets of recommendations. But this inevitably lacks a certain qualitative dimension; much depends upon the nature of the recommendation and whether it is a generalised one or very specific. Second, it is not always clear whether it was the committee's influence or another unacknowledged source which led to acceptance. Nor of course is it only government departments who exist to be persuaded. In the reports analysed here, major non-governmental bodies such as CEGB, BNFL, NIREX, English Heritage and the Welsh Water Authority not only gave evidence but responded positively to committee recommendations. So did quasi-government agencies administering legislative measures.

So in order to get a rounded view of the effectiveness of the new committee system it is necessary to complement the result of looking quantitatively at the fate of recommendations and to seek a more detailed account of the process from the varied and various interests with a stake in the outcomes. That is, to expose the interactions and negotiations which occur in the course of committee investigations.

Chapter 8 has established both a new approach to quantitative measurement of select committee effectiveness and the clear limits to the application of quantitative methodology to the concept of 'policy' and its development or mediation within a democratic pluralist system. There are strengths and weaknesses in any single data collection strategy and in this section a qualitative approach is adopted which poses problems of its own and requires a return to the concept of triangulation of data, thus permitting the evaluation to combine the strengths and correct some of the deficiencies of any one source of data, building in checks and balances and increasing the strength and vigour of our understanding of the impact of select committees.

In this way further insights are provided, some more subjective and intuitive measures, from the key actors in the process; for example, from the members themselves engaged at the heart of committee activity.

This technique of pluralistic evaluation draws heavily upon the theories of political pluralism which underlie the argument presented, identifying the range of interests and interpreting their separate notions of 'success', then attempting to disentangle the meanings of values brought to the process by each constituent stakeholder group, as it attempts to express its own perception in its own interest (Smith and Cantley, 1985).

Qualitative data in the form of words rather than numbers have been a staple tool of social science research for many years but in the past decade researchers in other fields such as public administration, sociology and policy analysis have shifted to a more qualitative paradigm (Miles and Huberman, 1985, p 15).

For the purposes of assessing select committee work, qualitative data have a particular attraction. They are a source of well-grounded rich description and explanations of processes occurring in localised contexts; often contexts not accessible to anyone other than participants - the 'sealed box' phenomenon discussed earlier.

Such data may also allow the research a degree of chronological flow and new theoretical integrations leading beyond initial preconceptions and frameworks. The viewpoint of the recipients or beneficiaries of policy - the stakeholders - can also be exposed with a vivid, meaningful flavour not easily reached by other means. As Smith (1978) has put it: "findings from interviews and other qualitative studies have a degree of undeniability".

Essentially this is a practical recognition that the student of the political effectiveness of select committees not only needs to be open to more than one way of looking at committees and their outputs and outcomes, but also needs an insurance against the possibility that preconceived ideas or enthusiasms colour the enquiry. The methodology, in short, ensures that we stand back from the consideration of success or failure of committee activity and ponder the multiple viewpoints from which such questions can be asked.

Different key actors require differing survey techniques; the earlier extended, in-depth conversation with a committee chair and officials ranged over both policy and process and their experience sustained over a whole parliament. In this chapter very specific questionnaires based upon the individual's own evidence and written submissions and the advice/recommendations they made have been used. A range of survey techniques have been utilised to match the particular category of participant, enabling us to focus sharply upon their own experience and then to reflect upon the consequences of their evidence. Thus the method used has been tailored to the role of the subject, ranging from those permanent participants whose involvement is sustained over a whole parliament and longer, through those who become intensely associated with the whole of one committee enquiry, to those witnesses who spend perhaps one concentrated four hour period answering questions in public session.

In order to reach the views of those most intimately involved in the political experience of formulating recommendations, nine MPs, each of whom had served on the Environment Committee, were approached; the sample was differentiated by party allegiance and by activity in three separate enquiries.   In the event six responded to postal questionnaires constructed to reflect their experience of specific topics and to elicit perceptions of outcomes, especially in the parliamentary arena.

Similar targeted surveys, built around particular memoranda and evidence were then directed to three pressure group witnesses, to three witnesses from economic self-interest groups and to two independent experts and laboratories.   These focused upon their own personal experience of the process and their reflective view of what subsequently transpired, both in policy terms and in the wider policy community.   Different committee reports were used for each of the interviewees.

Three specialist advisers, whose experience is sustained over the whole length of a particular investigation, took part in lengthy, face-to-face structured interviews at the end of which each completed a tick-sheet designed to ascertain their reflection of the outcome of their work in influencing the direction of policy and those who make it.

In this way the following pages attempt to "grasp the natives point of view" (Palmer, 1928; Burgess, 1982, p 107).

Committee members' perceptions

Six active members of the Environment Committee who had been intimately engaged in three of the most important investigations mounted during the parliament of 1983-87, were asked, for the purposes of this study, to reflect in retrospect on the impact of their reports: on acid rain (HC 446), radioactive waste (HC 191) and planning (HC 181).   What was their own measure of the impact their reports had on modifying the policy of the DOE?

Two members felt they had no influence, two thought they were very influential, and two 'moderately so'.   In terms of the score of accepted recommendations two MPs recorded the view that in these reports the level of acceptances represented failure, whilst others felt it was "all that could be expected" and one that the acceptance rate was highly successful.

Asked to assess the influence on the longer-term direction of Government policy, three members felt that their investigations had been moderately important in this regard, two very important and one "not in any way important".

In seeking to establish how these effects have been achieved, members were asked to consider the ways in which influence operates. Whilst none of them felt there would be immediate legislative change, two were convinced that change would derive from the committee's evidence improving the quality of the department's scientific knowledge, whilst five cited the select committee's ability to increase public awareness of environmental damage as the impetus to policy change. Three members said it was essentially long-term directions which would be modified and two registered the strengthened reputations of the ideological lobbyists derived from the quality of evidence they submitted.

Significantly, all six members supported the view that in due course Government would concede that a major new agency, coordinating all official activity to protect the environment, was the right response to the issues raised by the Environment Committee. All believed that the long-term, consistent and sustained programme of investigations undertaken by the committee would be the motivating force for such an outcome, thus echoing Rossi (1989a).

This survey also asked members of the Environment Committee to specify what influences, outside the committee activity, would have been more important in achieving change. The list they provided is a useful insight into the perception of MPs themselves, about the sources of pressure for policy change to which ministers and their advisers are susceptible. It comprises:

- parliamentary questions;

- opinion poll findings;

- pressure from the EC;

- pressure from foreign governments;

- "vested interests" (such as CEGB and BNFL).

Two of the six members questioned in this survey considered that no other influences are more important than select committee reports.

MPs were asked which sources of the evidence they heard influenced them most; contrary to the finding in Chapter 8, based on counts of inputs and citations, five of the six specified the evidence of independent experts as most important in shaping their recommendations. The sixth said that his overseas visits and conversations with foreign nationals, especially in the acid rain enquiry had most influence in forming his opinions. Members cited the disinterested or academic content of these witnesses' evidence as the basis for their view, echoing Rossi's view quoted above that MPs were wary of witnesses with a 'case' to pursue.

However, MPs are essentially creatures of party allegiance, and the way this fact affects their behaviour inside the committee needs to be explored.

The cross-party dimension

There is little doubt that concerns about the environment - about acid rain, CFCs, the ozone layer and nuclear waste - have, in the last decade, emerged from a fringe concern of the marginal 'greens' to an important and persistent theme of current political debate. These concerns are acknowledged daily in the media and given serious attention by leading political figures both in and out of government.   By the end of the 1980s the politics of the environment had, arguably, become the most prominent topic of debate with major conferences, media coverage and speeches from royalty, from the prime minister and other political leaders an everyday occurrence.   Much of the argument has been couched in non-party based terms.

The impetus for this growth, traced earlier in this book, has come from several sources.   The environmental lobby and the embryo Green political organisations represent one source; another is the EC; yet another is the sequence of tragic environmental disasters typified by Chernobyl, Bophal and Three Mile Island, in which the potentially world-wide scale of nuclear and chemical pollution has been indelibly imprinted on the public consciousness. But one of the factors which has ensured the success of this process is the role of the select committee system which has provided a new mechanism for bringing authoritative, well-researched commentary on current policy to the very heart of the parliamentary political process.

Back-bench MPs can speak with a new authority on matters of highly complex technical content, largely as a result of the methodical collection of data and examination of expert witnesses undertaken by select committees and the usually non-partisan, unanimous nature of the recommendations they make.   All of the MPs surveyed for this study indicated that they continue to pursue the topics they investigated as members of the Environment Committee, in other parliamentary activities. They form part of the back-bench resource whose expertise arises directly from the select committee system.

The absence of party ideology has been noticeable in the reports considered here, a point which some commentators have suggested allows the reference to all-party committees some additional credence. How much value, then, is there in the notion and does it lend a degree of authority to reports which partisan argument would not have?

In the cases under review it can be shown that not only was party interest of minimal concern, but that division of any kind was regularly negotiated in informal session. The evidence of Gren (1987) and of Rossi (1987) would appear to be confirmed by the following analysis. Table 14 shows that the ten reports produced on environmental topics during the parliament of 1983-87 contained 259 recommendations. Sixty-five amendments were proposed and of these more than half were withdrawn or agreed without division, leaving only 30 to go to formal division. It is some measure of the consensus achieved in these committees that only 11.5% of all recommendations were not fully supported. A total of 19 divisions occurred in which voting was straightforwardly Government supporters against the Opposition parties, and these were confined within three of the ten reports considered.

The substantial consensus achieved should not be confused with what Drewry and others have called 'the consensus model', in which committees collectively agree to undertake 'safe' or uncontroversial topics in order to avoid party-based splits (Drewry, 1985). This has not happened in the environmental debates examined for this study. Nor is Sir Hugh Rossi's determination to avoid the high profile topics the same thing. In fact, the tone of a number of the reports reviewed here is distinctly combative, and two of the three reports in which divisions occurred based on party lines (acid rain or radioactive waste) were the most challenging in tone and mode of investigation and were least well received by Government. In other words Conservative majority votes were certainly not necessarily in support of the Government on these issues.

Table 14: Formal amendments tabled in select committee proceedings: environmental reports 1983-87

	Formal amendments in select committee proceedings (environmental topics 1983-87)					
Topic	Committee recommendations	No of proposed	Amendments	Withdrawn	Agreed without division	Adopted or defeated on division
Green belt/land for housing HC 275 83/84	Environment	26	19	2	14	3
Acid rain HC 446 83/84	Environment	22	1	0	0	1
Wealth of waste HC 640 83/84	Trade and Industry	10	0	0	0	0
Wildlife and Countryside Act HC 6 84/85	Environment	18	2	0	2	0
Coastal pollution in Wales HC 101 85/86	Welsh Affairs	16	3	0	0	3
Radioactive waste HC 211 85/86	Environment	41	14	0	0	14
Planning: appeals, call-in and major public enquiries HC 181 85/86	Environment	37	22	4	9	9
Pollution of rivers and estuaries HC 183 85/86	Environment	36	0	0	0	0
Historic buildings and ancient monuments HC 146 86/87	Environment	42	4	0	4	0
Caravan Sites Act 1968 HC 414 84/5	Environment	11	-	-	-	-

It can be argued that a substantial degree of consensus is necessary if select committees are not to degenerate into miniature replays of battles on the floor of the House. This, however, has not resulted, in these investigations, in a blandness or marginality, or in deteriorating relationships with departments, as some commentators predicted (Drewry, 1985). Indeed one key actor in the process notes:

> Firstly, select committees are dealing largely with policy issues. Hence there is a growing relationship with the secretary of state. Civil servants appear as agents of the secretary of state. Second, most ministers have tended increasingly to ensure they carry the committee with them. The chairman and members of these committees have increased their influence with ministers and now acquire a good deal more official and unofficial information than they did in the past. (Cooper, 1987)

As has been seen, the environment as an area of policy development has moved centre-stage in the period covered by this enquiry, even accelerated in the following parliament, and the tone and content of many of the reports have confounded the critics of the select committee system who foresaw a cosy, non-partisan clique, remote from the real world. Certainly any impartial reader of the challenging enquiries described above would not agree to the term 'cosy', and the disposal of radioactive waste, for example, is as current and vital a policy issue of the real world as any now before parliament.

Perhaps the principal cause of the level of consensus demonstrated above is the perception within the committees themselves of their role, in the parliament of 1983-87, unique for its large Conservative majority and its unfettered use of prime ministerial power and drive, as being primarily one of dispassionate and constructive policy analysis and monitoring. Johnson concedes, in his most recent review:

> There are certainly specialised bodies which look with real gratitude to a committee for the evidence it has assembled and the issues it has highlighted. (Johnson, 1988, p 184)

The specialist advisers

Valuable insight into the political processes inside select committees can be gained from the specialist advisers appointed to assist in investigations. The ability of select committees to appoint such advisers derives from the recommendation of the Procedure Committee and in the standing orders of the House of Commons. The Liaison Committee has commended many committees for their 'imaginative use' of this facility (Drewry, 1985).

The Environment Committee has appointed appropriate specialists for each of its investigations who, by the nature of their role, provide a particularly valuable perspective on the effectiveness of investigations and the ability of members to get to grips with the complexities of subject matter. Advisers are independent, expert, and at the same time close observers of the members and of the way they use and interpret the information they gain.

This section draws on a piece of research comprising a series of structured interviews with three specialist advisers, attempting to draw qualitative assessments and additional insights via this participant observation. The comments of the three specialist advisers, appointed respectively for the investigations into planning (HC 181, 1986), acid rain (HC 446, 1984) and radioactive waste (HC 191, 1986) are summarised and examined in tabulated form (Table 15) with discussion, responses and comments under the more important headings, set out for each interviewee followed by commentary. The contributors to this exercise were a senior lecturer on environmental technology, a senior academic expert in planning law, and an independent consultant in radioactive science.

A prominent feature of these interviews, which each adviser acknowledged at least by implication, is that their involvement in the process, whilst neutral in a formal sense, is neither detached nor uncommitted. Advisers clearly have an influence, acknowledged or not, in the outcome of the process; each was responsible for recommending witnesses, for interpreting the meaning and weight of sometimes complex technical submissions. One explains: "I provided a layman's guide to the technical papers, reading, commenting and summarising. I prepared draft questions for members to pose to oral witnesses".

In the radioactive waste enquiry the adviser was asked to annotate the lengthier papers and to suggest new witnesses when pieces of evidence conflicted. All the advisers were present at deliberative meetings of the committees and were able to observe the process of arriving at recommendations. They saw no obvious party alignment in these sessions "apart from some occasional automatic gestures of opposition". Despite a unanimous view that the committee was under-resourced, all the advisers found the process positive and a good means - "perhaps the only means" - of exposing the scientific issues in a satisfactory public way.

One adviser noted a varying level of commitment among MPs observing that some would attend very briefly or fall asleep during sessions. Two found the chair oustanding in his grasp of detail and forensic ability. Those well-motivated members seemed driven by the desire to exercise some influence over policy and expressed some resentment that their ideas were so frequently dismissed out of hand by ministers. Asked about the distribution of power within the procedure one specialist adviser commented: "there is undoubtedly some power in knowledge but the chair and officers were quite clearly most influential forces". He felt at no time that he was persuading members to a view, or would have been successful if he had tried. He was kept a little at arms length from the committee and dealt mainly through officers. He did, however, have some influence on the direction of the enquiry by highlighting areas of controversy and argument between the scientists and within the industry (Patterson, 1988).

As to the influence of their own prejudices and whether they were influential as specialists, one expert responds:

> In the outcome, yes, better than I expected, but there was no conscious attempt to make this so. It happened because I was able to clarify for lay members what the evidence was saying, interpreted in the light of other evidence and highlight the key points. I had no influence on final recommendations other than helping to edit them for factual accuracy. (Patterson, 1988)

Another adviser comments:

> My earlier expectations of the report were limited but the distinctive virtue of select committee reports of this kind is that they are part of an educational process for civil servants within departments. They probably use them in internal arguments with their own advisers and this is more important than any residual influence on MPs or ministers. (Grant, 1988).

Table 15: Tabulated summary of interviews with three specialist advisers

	Adviser on radioactive waste (HC 191, 1986)	Adviser on planning (HC 181, 1986)	Adviser on acid rain (HC 446, 1984)
How were you appointed?	Informal approach based upon extant work. Had to be persuaded.	Soundings through RTPI. Informal approach first.	The DOE provided a list of names. Approached direct by clerk.
Was your experience negative or positive?	Apprehensive but ultimately positive.	Yes, good insight.	Outstandingly good.
Was it a good use of time?	Yes in due course.	Yes.	Yes.
What specific tasks were undertaken by you?	Prepared briefings for members. Commentary on evidence. Suggested witnesses and counter-witnesses. Checked draft recommendations. Consultations for clerks.	Suggested avenues of enquiry. Selection of witnesses. Deliberative meetings. Briefing for evidence sessions. Prepared questions.	Suggested witnesses. Prepared briefing document for members (a layman's guide). Reading submissions. Drafted questions. Comment on draft report.
Did you detect party divisions?	Not noticeable.	Minor gestures.	No strong divide.
What was the main motivation of committee members?	Not much. Some very lazy.	Resentment of government dismissal. Desire to influence policy.	Public concern fuelling concern.

	Adviser on radioactive waste (HC 191, 1986)	Adviser on planning (HC 181, 1986)	Adviser on acid rain (HC 446, 1984)
What were your general impressions of the committee process?	Under-resourced but good means of exposing issues. Members were of mixed ability.	Power and influence lay 80% with the chair and 20% with the clerk.	Positive force for good. Exposes scientific issues in the public interest. Got issue onto the political agenda.
What was your influence on the direction of the enquiry?	Minor.	None.	None.
What was your influence on the mode of enquiry?	None.	Some influence.	None.
What was your influence on the submission of evidence?	Significant.	Selection of issues.	Significant.
What was your influence on witnesses?	Some.	Some.	Some.
What was your influence on questions asked?	Significant.	Significant.	Some.
What was your influence on recommendations?	Accuracy only.	None.	Drafting only.
What was your influence on the ranking of evidence?	None.	[This interview was terminated early unavoidably.]	Strong influence.

	Adviser on radioactive waste (HC 191, 1986)	Adviser on planning (HC 181, 1986)	Adviser on acid rain (HC 446, 1984)
Were your own prejudices relevant?	In the event, yes, but mainly through clarifying what the evidence was saying.	[This interview was terminated early unavoidably.]	Inevitably, but not in any way contrary to witnesses or evidence.
What are your reflective comments on the report?	Had limited expectations. But distinctive virtue is in educating civil servants and government scientists. Issue and inconsistencies of policy well exposed. Compendium of basic technical information. One significant change of policy achieved.	A useful compendium of current knowledge. Good teaching aid to planning procedure. Well-researched. Welcomed by the institutes. Pressure groups gave very professional evidence.	An important and necessary job. Very influential in the wider policy community, especially in government research circles. A quite violent reaction from the CEGB and NCB at the recommendations.
What was your experience of contact with committee staff?	Very collaborative. My opinions sought frequently.	Close.	Most formal and infrequent.
Did you detect the 'delayed drop' phenomenon?	Yes.	[This interview was terminated early unavoidably.]	Yes. Impetus given to further research. Secondary influence of report not yet assessed.

	Adviser on radioactive waste (HC 191, 1986)	Adviser on planning (HC 181, 1986)	Adviser on acid rain (HC 446, 1984)
Do you agree that the purpose of the committee is to change the climate of opinion and to take rationality on board in a process which is essentially political?	Yes, and to identify conflicts of evidence and policy.	[This interview was terminated early unavoidably.]	Agree.
General comments	The nuclear industry was casual at first but later felt the need to be better prepared. The first few weeks evidence session appeared to be getting nowhere but after BNFL evidence which was dismissive, the whole thing took off: real team spirit. Government witnesses were least impressive. This was the first review of policy since 1974-76 (the Flowers Report). The enquiry exposed the fact that environment ministers were limited to issues of minimising waste. Wider nuclear policy is for the Department of Energy.	There was collaboration with the Department. They identified open doors on which to push. The report exposes differences in professional and legal circles and raised the level of the debate with all planning circles. Local authorities were the least effective part of the process. the report has heightened the awareness but the major policy issue concerning planning enquiries and public policy making is no nearer being resolved.	The European parliaments and pressure groups were very impressed. Hence HC 51 was published separately. The report also influenced pressure groups themselves; they have collaborated around the issue noticeably. The minister was a particularly impressive witness. Both the DOE and the industry saw this as an important inquisition of their conduct.

The three advisers were asked about the quality of the evidence and witnesses. One suggested that the departmental representatives were least prepared and weakest in presentation. Generally there was a high level of input and most of the pressure group witnesses were well respected and well received. Another said that the minister and his department prepared seriously and thoroughly for the acid rain enquiry and were particularly impressive in the evidence session at which they appeared.

The report on planning procedures was, in the expert adviser's view, very influential. The Government accepted, in one degree or another most of the committee recommendations, rejecting only five outright. Grant (1988) thought this was because they were very largely ones of an administrative kind. The DOE had set up its own internal review of procedures, rules and effectiveness, partly prompted by the knowledge that the committee was going to have an investigation. There was a lot of collaboration between the committee and the department and members were able to see many of the internal review papers. This may, in Grant's opinion, have determined the outcome of the generally favourable Government response, but major policy issues remain unresolved:

> The department were inspired to their own review by the knowledge that the committee were on to the subject; they saw it as an important inquisition of their own conduct of policy. Department witnesses prepared well and identified 'open doors' on which the committee need only push gently. Areas were identified where it appeared that Government would welcome committee recommendations. If not exactly a collaboration then a subtle process of joint encouragement! (Grant, 1988)

Likewise the acid rain report was "very influential" within the wider policy community. Within Government circles it resulted in more emphasis on research and more monitoring activity. The adviser notes the impact which the report made on European governments and particularly parliamentarians in Norway and Germany:

> They expected a party of British MPs to be unsympathetic to their case and were appreciative of the outcome and of the critical tone of the report. The fiercest contrary reaction came from the CEGB who were very volatile and saw it as an

inquisition of their conduct, reacting quite violently at a
scientific level against the recommendations. (Bell, 1988)

He underscores the importance of visits made to Europe and to
Galloway as having the greatest impact upon the members of the
committee:

Walking in dead forests and listening to the Norwegian
fishermen can make a stronger argument than a fifty page
technical paper. (Bell, 1988)

All three advisers played some part in the preparation of the final
report and recommendations of the committee investigations in
which they participated. One reports that he was consulted on
drafting, another edited the technical aspects of the
recommendations for factual accuracy, and the third contributed to
early drafting of recommendations prior to their approval. How did
they assess the impact which the final documents made? In the
case of scientific/technical issue type enquiries, perhaps the most
significant point about the role of specialist advisers is that they
improve the quality of the inquisition of scientific witnesses and
make it less likely that lay committee members will be bemused by
the complexity of the issues.

Each of the specialist advisers was asked to identify the extent
and nature of the influence which their reports had on Government
and the direction of policy. Each took part in an exercise in which
they indicated from the statements in Table 16 those which most
nearly summed up their views and the strength with which they
held that opinion. Table 16 below illustrates the result and provides
an interesting counter-point to the same subjects' comments in the
structured interview procedure. Each interviewee was asked to
mark only those statements which they believed to be true, and to
do so in one of three columns indicating the strength with which
they concurred. None marked statements implying that their
reports made no impression, or were unnoticed.

Table 16: Specialist advisers' assessment of select committee impact: 'which of the following statements most nearly represents your assessment of the impact of your select committee report, and how strongly do you hold that view?'

STATEMENT	BELIEVE STRONGLY	PROBABLY	POSSIBLY
Little or no impression upon either Minister or Department.			
Influenced other agencies involved in the policy or implementation process.		[acid rain] [radioactive waste]	
Changed the climate of opinion within the wider policy community.		[acid rain] [radioactive waste]	
Shifted the debate significantly forward.	[acid rain] [planning]	[radioactive waste]	
Made direct impact on current policy.	[acid rain]	[acid rain] [planning] [radioactive waste]	[radioactive waste]
Significantly affected subsequent policy development whether acknowledged or not.			
Will in due course form the basis of future policy change.			[radioactive waste]
Went virtually unnoticed.			

[acid rain] ACID RAIN [planning] PLANNING [radioactive waste] RADIOACTIVE WASTE

The acid rain report in the adviser's perception, then, made a significant impact on the policy community, on the progress of the debate and on the Government's policy development. There is less certainty of the success of the planning investigation but nevertheless the adviser notes the influence which the report had in shifting the debate on the issues forward. This compliments his earlier statement that the committee report formed a good compendium as a teaching aid, and as a summary of the issues at stake. The adviser's opinion that Government policy on radioactive waste is inconsistent and incoherent (Table 15, pp 154-57) perhaps leads to his rather more pessimistic assessment of the committee report's chances of influencing the debate or the participants; or of affecting future policy.

The independent experts

Table 13 (p 140) has demonstrated how substantial the notice taken of evidence to select committees is by those bodies or individuals categorised as 'independent experts': that is to say, those with no obvious economic self-interest or ideological position on the topic under scrutiny. Some such bodies, it is true, offer services as consultants and are active members of the policy community, but insofar as their evidence purports to be disinterested, factual and based upon professional expertise or academic knowledge in the field, their contribution is presented and accepted as that of experts. They were responsible for over 16% of the total 3665 inputs of evidence to the enquiries under review, and in the case of technical/scientific topics they represented 21% of all witnesses inputs, accounting for 21.5% of the citations in published committee reports. Their views of the effectiveness of select committees as agents of change are, therefore, of particular interest and the following comments are based on interviews with two such witnesses. They represented independent consulting laboratories, specialising in environmental engineering issues and are typical of the experts sought out by the committee clerk in a number of investigations.

The first, whose advice had been sought in more than one of the enquiries on environmental topics, commented on the quality of the inquisition when facing members:

> I found the committee searching in its inquiries; had a good appreciation of the complex issues surrounding the subject, and proposed a cohesive approach to improve standards etc. The select committee and the Royal Commission remain the most effective form of pressure to change Government policy - albeit a slow process.

This participant found it difficult to judge how far his advice had been taken specifically, but the concerns he had expressed in the field of waste disposal and contamination of land "are clearly reflected, both in the report and the department's response". His evidence in general, he scored as making "significant" impact, his specific memoranda were "moderately influential".

This witness and the second interviewee used the same term to describe their impact on the Government's response to the committee reports and both regard as "substantial" the select committee's contribution to the growth in parliamentary interest in environmental issues between 1983 and 1987, and believe that committee activity is an important element in stimulating policy change.

As long-term observers of environmental policy issues, both experts were asked to assess how far policy was likely to move towards committee recommendations in the longer term. They were certain it will; both were positive about the extent to which the reports were influential within the DOE, parliament and among practitioners and lobbyists.

These observers are perhaps in a stronger position to address longer-term outcomes than those with a campaigning commitment, and were asked to consider a longer perspective on committee impacts. One was convinced of their role in stimulating the growth of parliamentary interest in the environment: "an important element in the campaign to change policy in this area". He was less certain that the committee recommendations will eventually be reflected in specific Government policy, scoring "probably" to this question. However, the second records the view that the enquiries to which he contributed shocked the Government into devoting more resources to environmental issues: "they will try to pre-empt criticism of this kind in the future".

The self-interest lobby

The academic commentators of the 1970s argued that the accommodation of the 'purposeful aggregates' forming the powerful pressure groups were an essential part of pluralist democracy or, alternatively, part of the bargaining and incorporation of corporatist analysis (Rivers, 1974; Marsh, 1983; Richardson and Jordan, 1979).

However, in the Thatcherite climate of the late 1980s the role, particularly of the self-interest groups, required quite a different analysis. Marsh (1986) argues that the "drift and immobilisation of current policy making" could best be remedied by integrating pressure groups more effectively and comprehensively into the policy-making process via select committees.

Whilst nothing in Marsh's research suggests that this is, in fact, happening, the potential power and highly professional approach over many years, of such groups as the NFU, the CBI and House Builders Federation (HBF) has, with the growth of the select committee system, been brought to bear in the interest of their members, where they see their vital interests at stake. If such bodies had lost some of their 'insider' status with government departments, they have been welcomed into the committee rooms on a regular basis, not least in the debates on environmental issues such as those discussed here. For this study, the view of three bodies contributing both memoranda and evidence to the Environment Committee's pollution of rivers and estuaries and planning appeals investigations, were sought. Their impressions of the committee, the outcome and their assessment of the importance in policy formation terms, of the reports are examined below.

Compared with the other groups of participants recorded in this chapter there is a distinctly less enthusiastic assessment of the role of the Environment Select Committee from all three of the major representative groups who responded to questionnaires related to the evidence they gave and the technical memoranda they supplied. The HBF, the CBI the NFU each recorded their opinions in the targeted survey that their own contribution had minimal or no effect and that the committee report itself was either "moderately" influential or not so at all.

The HBF specified three of the nine recommendations it put to the committee as having emerged as policy or in Government White Paper proposals in the three years following the select committee report, but recognised that other influences within the policy community had contributed to the outcome.

Whilst the CBI registered the view that select committees are a moderately important element in the process of policy development on environmental topics, the NFU and HBF thought they had no influence. However, the latter two bodies stated that river pollution policy might move closer to the committee's recommendations over time but the initiative to privatise the industry had been announced whilst the investigation was in progress and had overtaken the debate. This, they thought, ensured that there would be a welcome only for those committee recommendations which coincided with Government policy. This comment echoes the assessment of Judge that Government will be receptive of fresh perspectives when these do not challenge its own "ideological certainties" (Judge, 1990).

Of the three respondent bodies, two believed the select committee had made no contribution to DOE thinking. The HBF thought that the report on planning appeal issues influenced the DOE but made no impact in parliament or in the building industry. However, all three were of the view that committee reports made an impact among environmentalists.

It was the direct experience of committee proceedings which produced the most critical comment from these witnesses. The HBF spokesperson comments that MPs did not appear to understand the evidence, were more interested in "short-term political goals", and the proceedings were too party-political in tone:

> Committees will not really be effective unless they learn from US congressional committees, eschew party dogma and acquire some research capacity. (HBF, 1989)

In consequence, the approach to taking part in select committee enquiries, in the HBF view, is to accept that the real audience is the DOE. Department officials will respond directly to the points made in committee by representative bodies on important points. This is perhaps an indication that the great national interest groups, who no longer have quite the same 'insider' status of the pre-1979 days, are finding other means of communication not only with Government but with other agencies too. Contrary to Marsh's hypothesis (see p 165) this witness affirms:

> Select committees are not a mechanism for talking to others in the policy community. We have our own means of pursuing the debate. (HBF, 1989)

Thus in both process and outcome, the participants who have been characterised here as having a direct self-interest, or who formally represent an economic interest, perceive the committee role as marginal. In terms of Nixon's view of committees as "climate changers", or Marsh's proposition that they have the function of "linking organised groups and departments of state more closely to the parliamentary system", it would appear that this group of witnesses take a less sanguine view than the other groups examined here (Nixon and Nixon, 1983; Marsh, 1986). It may be significant that these bodies which were so powerful in the corporatist context of a decade earlier, had not yet come to terms with the style of 'executive leadership' which the Thatcher Governments have exhibited in the 1980s.

The HBF comment on MPs bears directly on the discussion by Judge (1983) of the specialisation and expertise of MPs. Judge draws the distinction between "specialist knowledge", and the process of specialising in a policy area without necessarily being an expert. But a further distinction which emerges in this instance suggests that committee members who specialise in environmental issues may lack any understanding of the manufacturing, farming or construction problems faced by those industries also engaging with pollution issues.

The pressure groups

In the previous chapter it has been illustrated how specific pressure group recommendations fare in the select committee system, but in the underlying relationships which are forged, there is an element of ambivalence which Porritt makes explicit, and which illustrates the hesitation of some nationally-known issued-based bodies about entering whole-heartedly into the environment of the Westminster political system:

> Friends of the Earth now contribute evidence to every single committee enquiry and we're getting to the stage where we have to be terribly, terribly careful. Because those committees are fierce, and rightly so. If you muck it up and get your facts wrong, or you turn out and you sound thin, it's

> very bad for the credibility of the organisation.   (Porritt, 1988)

In contradiction Greenpeace, who on two occasions have had public quarrels with the Environment Committee over questionable evidence (radioactive waste), and leaked documents (acid rain), are pragmatic about their appearances:

> Governments listen to us less and less, but if we can make a case at committee and register a detailed scientific basis for it, published in HMSO papers, then we are at least on the record in a way which we have not achieved before. (Greenpeace, 1988)

These insights suggest that the question of incorporation of interest groups is a two way issue. Those with an ideological case are wary of too close an identification with the political system they seek to influence in just the same way as committee members are about accepting their evidence (see Rossi, 1987).

Another nationally respected body, the CPRE, indicate a different view of the relationship. Their experience suggests that there is a sense in which the select committee is scrutinising not only the DOE, but the ideas of other groups within the policy community who are, in giving evidence, actually testing the credibility of their own views and ideas. The chief planning officer of the CPRE, whose evidence is quoted earlier, comments:

> Select committees offer the opportunity too, for organisations like CPRE to present a particular vision to independent scrutiny.   It [The Environment Committee report into planning] provided a basis for further work by CPRE and a climate of opinion in which CPRE's views are likely to flourish.

This is an example of Marsh's proposition that the process of giving evidence to committees in some way changes the participant groups. It appears also to improve the group's own understanding of public policy issues.

Analysis of CPRE's detailed evidence on planning procedures suggests that it was significant, identifying five specific recommendations out of fourteen which CPRE put forward, that were reflected in the committee's report (HC 181, 1986). The same recommendations appear in the Government's response (Cm43) only on a 'moderate' level.

Summary

This chapter has sought to elicit a qualitative dimension to the work of select committees, from the multiple viewpoints of those who have participated in the process. The impressionistic and practical judgements of people, ranging from the long-term participants to those having a brief encounter, whether as expert witness or suppliants, advisers or voting members, bring a valuable insight to the evaluation process.

It is significant that almost none are willing to discount the committee role in influencing policy. Whether from the perspective of a particular topic or as a spokesperson for an ongoing interest, or an adviser or expert witness, the responses to our questionnaires record a level of consistency which amounts to an impressive body of support for the role which back-bench parliamentarians are carving out. Even the more sceptical comments from representatives of capitalism recorded above are tempered by the knowledge that the style of executive leadership established by the then prime minister did not afford better opportunities to exert influence (Judge, 1990).

The attempt in this chapter to bring together a small but diverse range of opinion from participant observers is designed to give depth and leaven to the quantitative assessment of earlier chapters. It is, in the end, the impressions and assessments of those who take part, however peripherally, in the drama of political action, which will determine the weight and significance that history places upon the committee process. At the very least it is a central piece of the jigsaw.

The explosion of interest, since 1987, in environmental dangers to the planet has meant that every agent, whether of capitalistic endeavour, policy maker, lobbyist or state action must now be aware of, have an opinion about, or feel a responsibility for what he or she does and says. In that sense their assessments of perhaps brief and fleeting experience at the epicentre of power and decision making are a valid part of the attempt to assess what Nixon and Nixon (1983) term the attempt to change the climate in which policy is made. Before going on to draw together these disparate viewpoints, and the quantitative assessment of the previous chapter, the next chapter turns to an examination of other kinds of reactive, repercussive and less obvious consequences of committee investigations which this project has exposed, and to a discussion of assessing their importance.

ten

CONTINGENT RESPONSIVENESS TO COMMITTEE ACTIVITY

Introduction

The key question for most academic observers, and indeed for participants in the select committee process is: 'do they influence policy development?' It has been evident from the major studies reviewed here that the question remains open (Marsh, 1986; Drewry, 1989). All suggest, however, that there is significant evidence to establish the affirmative case.

As Drewry's updated study comments:

> The short-term impact of committees - as crudely measured by Governmental U-turns and ministerial climb-downs - was in this parliament (save in cases rare as to underline the generality of the rule) as slight as it had been in 1979-83. (Drewry, 1989)

But this is hardly to the point and he goes on to concede that committees are indeed significant and that the concept of success and failure in government is complex.

The multiplicity of ways in which committees influence policy and practice goes far wider than a narrow definition of 'Government policy'. There is an interesting parallel to be drawn between committee recommendations and those produced by the Central Policy Review Staff (CPRS) up to its abolition in 1983. A study of CPRS reflecting on success and failure, by two of its leading participants says:

perhaps the most successful CPRS reports have been those that were rejected because they were 'ahead of their time'.

The aim should be to put new items on the agenda and change the way people think inside and outside government. This is a slow and painful process. Most major proposals made by a body like CPRS sink like a stone at first and will then take at least two or three years to re-surface. When they do, sometimes disconcertingly modified, they will be claimed, without attribution, by other people. (Blackstone and Plowden, 1980)

In this chapter that theme is pursued concentrating particularly on some of the unexpected ways in which committee activity has demonstrably influenced, changed or created policy and action; has had repercussions in unconventional or unanticipated ways; or has opened up potential for progress in terms not immediately measurable, but clearly to be put in the balance on the side of 'success'.

The 'delayed drop' phenomenon

A number of witnesses and key actors in this discussion have referred to what is here termed the 'delayed drop'; in other words the tendency for recommendations of a committee to be rejected or ignored by departments (or, in one major instance referred to below, a nationalised producer) only to appear at some time in the future as policy or action. The extent to which the modification can be traced to the influence of the original committee recommendation is often minimal. The extent to which the committee argument stimulated the process of change may not be measurable but it is too frequent an occurrence, and too often remarked, to ignore as a possible product of select committee influence.

Another aspect of the same phenomenon is the tendency for the select committee debate to stimulate change and development within the policy community irrespective of any action by Government; for the practitioners to take on the colours, chameleon-like, of the committee report unilaterally. The stake-holding professionals responsible for practice and implementation may not wait for legislative change but by dint of debate and acceptance arising from committee recommendations, may roll forward policy within the sub-regional, inter-organisational networks in a way which pre-empts official departmental legitimation. Some prime examples of these tendencies are discussed below, both from the environmental reports utilised in this study and from other areas of policy.

The case of the flue gas desulphurisation retro-fit

One of the most important recommendations of the Environment Committee's report on acid rain (HC 446 1983/4) was that which addressed the need for the CEGB and industry to reduce the emission of SO_2 and NO_x by the retro-fitting of flue gas desulphurisation (FGD) equipment to power stations and plant.
In its response in December 1984 the Government said:

> The inspectorates have judged that abatement is not possible because of ... the high costs involved. This would add some 5% to electricity bills.

> The Government believes that there are good prospects that new and better combustion technologies will lead to reductions. ... In these circumstances the Government does not intend to commit the country to expensive emission controls. (Cmnd 9397)

In November 1985 the minister of state for the environment and the parliamentary under-secretary for energy appeared again before the committee to reiterate that policy. However, in March 1986 the minister (Mr Waldegrave) announced that there would be a review of policy.
The CEGB, in submitting evidence to a new investigation on air pollution, undertaken by the Environment Committee, announced that it had in fact now, "with a new scientific understanding", decided to launch a programme of FGD retro-fit to the larger power stations. The cost would be £600 million at 1986 prices, and the decision had been made in June 1986, that is to say seven months after the minister had told members there would be no policy change (see CEGB evidence to the Committee: HC 270, 1988, vol II, p 53).

The growth of urban development corporations

The Environment Committee's report on the green belt and land for housing (HC 275, 1984) recommended the setting up of more Urban Development Corporations (UDCs) to ensure that if local authorities were slow to reclaim and bring derelict land into development, then these Governmental agencies could do the job for them.

In its response (HC 635, 1984; Hansard, 1984) the Government said that it thought these bodies, which had been set up for London Docklands and for Merseyside, were "the exception rather than the rule", and it would be neither justifiable or practical to set up more. In fact by 1987 a further five UDCs had been established in major cities, and the Conservative manifesto for the 1987 election introduced a proposal for setting up non-elected private bodies, with similar powers, to take over inner city housing estates, and derelict land for refurbishment and onward sale.

Powers to create these bodies, with functions modelled on UDCs, were provided in the 1988 Housing Act, and six announced in January 1988, named Housing Action Trusts (HATs).

Charges for planning appeals

Another important recommendation of HC 181 (1986) was that if developers pursued planning applications which were unreasonable and were refused by the secretary of state on appeal, all the local authority's costs should be awarded against the appellant company. Similarly where an authority refused consent on land where there was a presumption of development, the authority should bear all the costs of a successful appeal. The minister's response was to uphold the view of the Council on Tribunals that costs should not be awarded except where one of the parties had behaved unreasonably.

In 1987, however, the DOE introduced revised criteria (circular 2/87) and using powers under Section 42 of the Housing and Planning Act 1986, has provided that costs can be recovered of the entire enquiry including administrative costs and departmental overheads (S1 No. 1787 dated 17 November 1988).

Another recommendation which CPRE put to the committee (rec 38) was that developers should not be allowed to hold appeals in abeyance without good reason. This proposal finally appeared in a Government consultation paper in 1989, four years on (see 'Efficient planning: a consultation paper', DOE 28 July 1989).

Action stimulated within the policy community

Instances of the recommendations of committees gaining an indifferent reception from the parent department but creating profound and positive reactions from those policy stake-holders who are responsible for implementing policy are equally difficult to measure.

One such instance is the February 1989 report of the Environment Committee on toxic waste (HC 22, 1989) which had recommended the end of dumping toxic waste in the North Sea. Government's half-hearted endorsement of the sentiment (Cm 679 para 4.20) promised no immediate action. However, within four months of the committee report's publication, one of the largest UK chemical industries, ICI, announced the investment of £35 million to eliminate the disposal into the North Sea of its methyl methacrylate wastes and to go for recycling instead.

The committee clerk to the Social Services Committee comments on a somewhat similar example arising from her committee's 1985 report on community care which had sought to establish a policy underpinning for this initiative. The 'Care in the community' report had constituted an important attempt to identify and define the limits and standards for implementing this action, but had been poorly received by the DHSS. Irwin comments that the report nevertheless had proved invaluable to practitioners throughout the National Health Service and had become a 'bible' for social workers and departments throughout the country (Irwin, 1988).

That these kinds of innovation happen is undoubted, and the examples discussed here are a small sample of those littered through the recent history of select committee activity. It is not without significance that all three specialist advisers interviewed in Chapter 9 indicated that longer-term unacknowledged policy changes probably took place (see Table 16, see p 160). To find an explanation for them is more difficult and to fit them into any neat and clear-cut model of policy change is a risky enterprise, especially where the ideological thrust of Government is simple and direct. Nevertheless, they offer an insight into the way committee reports take on a meaning and importance outside the immediate policy debate and address a wider constituency than the House, the minister, or the department to whom they are addressed. These examples illustrate continuities within British political life which persist, often discreetly, in order to avoid what Deakin (1986) has termed the "stigma of consensus".

The explanation may lie in a closer understanding of the nature of alliances between agents within the system and the activities of those who utilise the work of select committees to pursue initiatives of their own. Alliances are a particularly interesting area of development arising from the new select committee system. Those within the Whitehall environment seeking change or opposing vested interests may encounter road blocks thrown up by those interests and reach out for collaborations which will keep their proposal alive or supply crucial additional arguments. Those whom Deakin (1986) terms "policy entrepreneurs" will cultivate sympathetic bureaucrats or quango technocrats much as those on the outside have traditionally sought to do. Select committees and their investigations represent so far understated opportunities for such alliances in a pluralist democracy, and indeed may be at the root of the phenomenon of policy change via the 'delayed drop'.

Committee enquiry as the spur to action?

One of the less obvious aspects of the ambivalent relationship between a select committee and the department it monitors is the tendency, referred to by more than one key participant in this study, for departmental officers to anticipate the investigation, once announced, or for ministers to pre-empt a committee report by early announcement of new policy.

We have noted that the DOE produced a consultative paper on water privatisation just as the Environment Committee had got its enquiry into the pollution of rivers and estuaries under way. Both Rossi (1987) and Gren (1987) refer to the increase in activity which is noticeable within the appropriate section of the DOE once a new investigation is announced. Similarly Barrett has observed the tendency for the good departmental civil servant to welcome select committee investigations on the grounds that it will allow him/her to press issues which had failed to get support earlier, or to argue for innovation "on the back of the committee report" (Barrett, 1989).

How far can this phenomenon of committee as 'spur to endeavour' within departments be quantified? For the purposes of this study an output monitoring exercise was devised, based upon the output/activity of one section of the DOE that deals with waste management policy, before and during the Environment Committee enquiry into toxic waste, undertaken between May 1988 and January 1989 (HC 22, 1989).

In the five and a half years between 1983 and the announcement of the committee's enquiry, the policy output, measured in terms of published advice, legislative proposals and consultative papers issued by the Waste Management Unit of the DOE, amounted to six items: one per annum. In the ten months from the start to the completion of the enquiry, the same unit issued ten items: one per month (see Table 17).

This disparity indicates at the very least a marked upsurge of activity once the enquiry was launched and perhaps an attempt to anticipate the highly critical tone of the committee's subsequent report, which said:

> never, in any of our enquiries into environmental problems, have we experienced such consistent and universal criticism of existing legislation and of central and local government as we have during this enquiry. (HC 22, 1989, p xi)

The committee chair, Sir Hugh Rossi, confirms the impression that the investigation was a spur to action:

> Our progress over a period of ten months was marked by regular announcements of new Government initiatives or the issue of consultative documents and the thrust of our examination of witnesses became clear. If we achieved nothing else we at least stimulated departmental action. (Rossi, 1989b)

There is no obvious other reason for this upsurge of activity, no demands from the EC, no new parliamentary or electoral programme; indeed the legislation demanding special waste disposal authority management plans was 14 years old. One committee witness characterised the production of the consultation paper on the role of Waste Disposal Authorities (WDAs) (Jan 1989) on the day before the minister was due to give evidence as "provocative":

> The production of such an important consultation paper leaving the committee very little chance to read it before the minister gave evidence could be accounted as either an outrageous piece of cheek, or as a move of such finesse that Machiavelli must have revolved, giggling in his grave. (Hawkins, 1989)

Table 17: **Policy output: Department of the Environment Waste Management Unit published output 1983-87 and May 1988 - March 1989**

The six years 1983-1987

Waste management papers

Waste management paper 25 - clinical wastes	1983
Waste management paper 24 - cadmium bearing waste	1984
Waste management paper 8 - heat treatment cyanide wastes (2nd edition)	1985
Waste management paper 26 - landfilling wastes	1986

Major consultation papers/draft legislation

Waste disposal law amendments consultation Paper	Sept 1986

Legislation

Control of pollution (landed ships waste) regulation	Mar 1987

The ten months May 1988-March 1989

Waste management papers

Waste management paper 24 (revised)	Oct 1988
Waste management paper 27	Jan 1989

Major consultation papers/draft legislation

Waste disposal law amendments: conclusions	June 1988
Waste disposal law amendments: follow-up consultation paper	Nov 1988
Integrated pollution control: a consultation paper	July 1988
Role and function of WDAs: a consultation paper	Jan 1989

Legislation

Transfrontier shipment of waste regulation	June 1988
The collection and disposal of waste regulations	May 1988
The control of pollution (special waste) (amendment) regulations	Oct 1988
The control of pollution (landed ships waste) (amendment) regulations	Feb 1989

This evidence, whilst perhaps illustrating an extreme and quantifiable example of departmental activity in response to committee investigative enterprise, is mirrored in many of the accounts of other investigations especially those conducted in challenging mode.

For example, reference to the DOE publications catalogues show that items on radioactive waste increased over 1000% in the period of the select committee investigation:

1982/83	6
1983/84	6
1984/85	61
1985/86	7

The committee investigation was announced in 1984 and published in January 1986 (HC 191, 1986).

Raising the profile

The power of select committees to draw attention to a topic or to raise its profile in political terms deserves attention. It will be recalled that Porritt, for example, comments that the first indication of an awareness of green issues within the Conservative party dates from the time that the Environment Committee took up the acid rain issue in 1984 (HC 446). How far can this be verified or quantified and is it true of other issues and other kinds of committee?

Acid rain, a relatively unfamiliar term in the early 1980s, had been identified by scientists but had not been widely understood outside the EC environment lobby and the campaigning literature of conservationists and ecologists. As a political issue it did not exist until four parliamentary events occurred in 1984:

May 1984	The Environment Committee opened an enquiry into acid rain and took public evidence in weekly sessions until July.
8th June 1984	A House of Commons debate took place upon an EC Directive on emissions from power stations.
December 1984	The Government's response to the acid rain report was published.

11th January 1985 House of Commons debate on the Environment Committee report.

It is on the floor of the House that the political profile of an issue is truly established and Figure 12 charts the growth of the subject of acid rain, expressed in terms of debates, parliamentary questions and ministerial statements.   By charting the number of these mentions in each parliamentary session before, during and after the select committee report and the Government's response, it is possible to illustrate the increase in profile of this topic in relation to the period of the committee enquiry and report, and the two debates which took place.

It is not possible to establish absolute cause and effect, and indeed the interest among European governments in acid rain and the early campaigns of the environmental pressure groups may have been contributory factors.   However, an analysis of the parliamentary questions asked and the members asking them does suggest that there is a direct relationship between the activities on the committee corridor and those in the chamber.

The ability of select committees to get topics debated in the House during the parliament of 1983-87 was significantly better than in their first term (1979-83). In addition to the three estimates days set aside for committee reports (topics chosen by the Liaison Committee),   there   were   adjournment   debates,   Government motions, opposition day debates and second reading debates during which committee reports were introduced.   The Environment Committee achieved eight debates, as follows:

4 July 1984	Department of Environment main estimates Property Services Agency main estimates
11 January 1985	Acid rain report
11 July 1985	Department of Environment main estimates Property Services Agency main estimates
13 May 1986	Radioactive waste report
24 June 1986	Department of Environment main estimates Property Services Agency main estimates (HC 356)

Figure 12: Acid rain - growth in parliamentary activity related to committee enquiry period

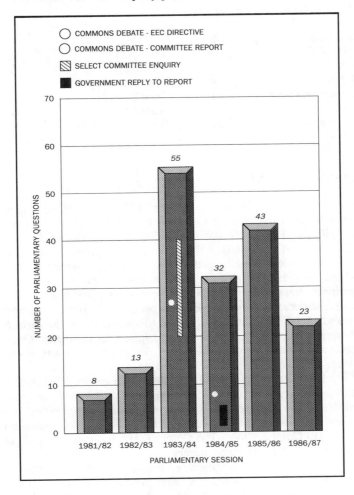

The number of other departmental select committee reports debated on the floor of the House, or at least reaching the order paper in the 1983-87 parliament are as follows:

Agriculture	0	Energy	4
Scottish Affairs	0	Transport	2
Defence	7	Foreign Affairs	6
Social Services	4	Treasury and	
Education and Science	1	Civil Service	15
Trade and Industry	4	Home Affairs	0
Employment	54	Welsh Affairs	0

A conduit for Europe

When Mr Stanley Clinton Davis, the EC commissioner, gave evidence to the Environment Committee's investigation into toxic waste (HC 22, 1989), the chair remarked that it was an historic occasion, since it was the first time that the European Commission had submitted itself to interrogation by a national parliament.

Whilst this is not strictly true, it was a novel event for Westminster and perhaps it would be more to the point to say that it was the first occasion when the EC had been able to put its policies, plans and legislative strategy directly to members of the British parliament, seeking to gain back-bench support for measures which in some cases the Executive had been distinctly lukewarm about adopting.

The formal platforms for the British parliament to consider EC measures are embodied in the terms of reference of two committees: the House of Commons Select Committee on European Legislation and the House of Lords Select Committee on the European Communities. The Commons committee, comprising 16 members, produces large numbers of reports each year (see Table 18 below), but does little more than list the draft directives, draft regulations, amendments and other instruments coming out of Brussels, indicating which, in their opinion, are politically or legally important enough to be considered by the House. At any one time up to 200 such instruments recommended for further consideration will be outstanding; some for eight or more years (HC 22, 1989, vol xx, p xiii). The practical difficulties inherent in this task have been discussed fully in Ryle and Richards (1988).

The Lords select committee operates through a number of sub-committees and is, in the view of Hayward and Norton (1986), an authoritative and effective scrutineer of European measures, proving more effective than its Commons counterpart. Its reports are substantial and examine single issues in depth, frequently summoning witnesses from the ranks of Commission officials (see Table 18).

Table 18: Reports to parliament by Commons and Lords select committees on European legislation 1983/84 - 1987/88

Session	Commons select committees	Lords select committees
1983/84	35	27
1984/85	31	16
1985/86	29	24
1986/87	20	9
1987/88	39	22

The minor historic incident above, which happened after the period of this book's concern, is however an example of the ability of departmentally based scrutiny committees to open up a quite different window on to Westminster/Whitehall processes for the benefit of European politicians and policy makers, both within and outside the EC, and quite outside the formal intercourse of national governments.

If the transportation and disposal of toxic waste is a trans-frontier problem, then in every respect the 1984 enquiry into acid rain was the forerunner of all the later examples of the need for closer international cooperation on continental pollution issues. It was that report (see Porritt, 1988) which focussed public attention on the interdependence of nations in seeking solutions, both political and technical, to the global threat.

After publication of the acid rain report (HC 446, 1984) a number of politicians from Norway, West Germany and the EC wrote detailed responses, supporting the select committee and regretting that the UK Government has not felt able to support the important recommendation to join the '30% club' (see Chapter 7, case study II). These interventions were subsequently published in a follow-up report (HC 51, 1986), suggesting new avenues for collaboration and alliances between back-bench scrutiny bodies and other national parliaments, many of whom see themselves as victims of exported British pollution.

As such it is an illustration of the power of committees to create linkages which may not be of major significance, or quantifiable, but clearly add a qualitative underpinning to the argument for committee influence on environmental policy development, bringing to issues which are so often transnational in context, an ability for other national parliamentarians to join the debate within Westminster. If the issue is international, then so is the debate. Alliances across national frontiers between parliamentarians postulate an exciting potential not exploited in the intervening years.

Summary

The general approach to this chapter has been to assume that the search for 'success' would be more thorough if supported by data from differing sources and from a triangulation of research methods. The quantitative approach, assisted by a matrix of key elements, has been tested to its limits and has been enriched by the techniques of pluralist evaluation and by formal and informal interviews. Richness and variety has been maximised, even at the expense of some 'rigour'.

The debate about quantitative versus qualitative data collection has, in a sense, been proved artificial since this study is at pains to make clear that an understanding of the effectiveness of select committee activity relies both on precise numerical data and on intuitive and interpretive insights of those involved. It has been possible to demonstrate, for example, that even in those investigations conducted in a 'challenging' mode, in which the apparent level of success is lowest, subsequent actions and later policy changes such as those described above, seem to demonstrate that committee influence is a far more subtle phenomenon than any quantitative count of recommendations would imply.

In the final part of the study further theoretical dimensions are examined and there are reflections on the case studies and research findings and their implications for the future of select committees. The robustness of the matrix approach is tested on the work of other committees and other policy arenas. There is an examination of the wider constitutional framework of scrutiny of the Executive and some tentative judgements are made both about the importance of the system and the directions it must take if the concept of back-bench policy making is to have any meaning.

eleven

THE LIMITS OF COMMITTEE INFLUENCE

Introduction

The purpose of the remainder of this study is to reflect, not only on current success and failure, but to examine the practical and theoretical implications which must be understood if the committee system is to develop a more substantial role. Whether the matrix approach has a plausibility on a wider canvas than has been considered so far is also discussed.

The attempt to prise open the sealed boxes of the parliamentary system and to look at one aspect of the making of public policy has further illuminated the complex nature of the whole process. In looking at the role of select committees the futility of relying upon one structure of policy making as the ideal to be aimed at can be demonstrated. It may be, in agreement with Dror, that because there are so many barriers in the way of rational policy making, that the limits of both rational and incremental debates have been reached; and to paraphrase Dror, have sought to find balances between information and intuition, guess and estimate, measurement and impression (Dror, 1973, p 158).

The making of public policy - and in this case the 'greening' of public policy - is certainly no field of study for those with a low tolerance for ambiguity. The policy-making system is, to paraphrase Dror again, only a sub-system of society and interacts constantly with culture, public opinion, social groups, economic, religious and all other institutions; all components of society.

The case has been made that the select committee is a mechanism for achieving that interaction; a multi-dimensional instrument for evaluating and improving real policy making. It is located firmly in the pluralist framework and should be recognised for its dependable capability for analysis, diagnosis and critique, and for the near-centrality of its siting within the democratic functioning of a free parliament. Ironically, the select committee may be most necessary when strains on that freedom are greatest.

How then can its role be strengthened, its influence be underpinned? How can its place in the constitutional framework of government be established without equivocation?

Perhaps a key point of this study of select committees and environment policy is that committees have been gathering facts, scrutinising actions, criticising and advising departments largely in areas where policy has been in flux (for example, where new scientific problems and new technical advances have been emerging). The frontiers of knowledge about radioactive waste, about pollution of the oceans, and the destruction of the ozone layer, have been advancing faster than policy can be made, and select committees - especially the Environment Committee - have been at the leading edge of these debates. Indeed it would be true to say that without the platform of an Environment Committee investigation such as that into radioactive waste, many of the issues would not have been raised at all in the context of Westminster policy making (Patterson, 1988). In these technical/scientific topics especially, the contribution of committee reports in informing MPs and in the formation of policy, rather than the ex post-facto scrutiny of existing policy, has been demonstrably present, whether acknowledged or not.

It is this role in policy formulation which Marsh's 1986 study was advocating but was unable to find when he argued that committees should act as "independent agents in a more plural policy-making structure" (Marsh, 1986, p 64).

There is a contrast between the undoubted growth of expertise in the surveillance of the Executive under the committee system, and the increasingly authoritarian Conservative administrations of the 1980s, which McAuslan has suggested represented a "gallop towards elective dictatorship" (McAuslan, 1989). This contradiction provides the essential abrasiveness which must be understood more clearly and examined for a wider application than has been possible thus far. "When committees bite, ministers increasingly feel the need to bark back" said a recent commentator, and the growth of that tendency will be traced well beyond the boundaries of environmental concerns (Wintour, 1988).

The parliamentary critics who opposed the new system in 1978 were worried that committees would diminish the essential clash of political debate on the floor of the House and would somehow sully the purity of ideological struggle with their consensus politics. This prediction needs to be examined more than a decade on.

There is a sense in which the impetus for the select committee system derived from the failure of the 1970s devolution debate. Now, the Labour Opposition's renewed interest in devolution and regionalism as an antidote to elective dictatorship is just one strand of the argument for changes in institutional and administrative arrangements that commentators are urging upon the legislature. These arguments are examined in the following pages for the role which select committees might play, with particular reference to the closer links with the EC and the need to find more efficient means of scrutinising Community legislation. This discussion leads to the need for further theoretical underpinning and an examination of the link between committees and what Rhodes (1981) has called "sub-central governments" and Westminster policy makers.

The concept of the select committee as agent for linking organised and often conflicting interests to departments of state and tabling their concerns in a public and accountable way, described in earlier chapters, is significant because the process requires that both departments and lobbyists examine the issues from the perspective defined by the committee (Judge, 1990). This role is perhaps not so much to do with the process of parliament, as with the creation of informed public debate based on a wider canvas than either the Executive or the interest groups would separately allow.

A later chapter is concerned to examine possible futures for the select committee system. If it is, indeed, the strongest constitutional mechanism for scrutiny and the best hope for exercising a more rigorous oversight of the Executive, what more needs to be done to achieve what a leading authority has described as:

> the unlimited character of the claim for information, a fundamental parliamentary right of the highest importance ... which, both constitutionally and practically is a condition precedent to all efficient parliamentary government. (Redlich and Ilbert, 1908, vol II, p 40)

The same authority added that the powers both as exercised by the House and its select committees are circumscribed by "qualifications, apparent contradictions and lack of opportunity to exercise the powers which undoubtedly exist". The extent to which the current committee system has leapt these hurdles or can be equipped so to do needs to be examined.

A taxonomy of influence

The spectacular explosion of interest in environmental pollution, especially in acid rain, the depletion of the ozone layer, poisonous waste and the greenhouse effect, has been given added impetus by a number of well-publicised events. In the summer of 1988 an Italian freighter spent months attempting to offload a cargo of toxic waste from Nigeria, only to be turned away by many European port authorities. An epidemic of viral illness killed thousands of grey seals around the coasts of Europe and was said to be the result of pollution of the North Sea. Scientists predicted that further depletion of the ozone layer in the atmosphere would result in widespread skin cancers in the human population in the 21st century (Jones, 1988). In the same year the prime minister made a series of speeches both at home, and in Europe, pledging Government action and a new emphasis for policy. In two by-elections at Govan and Epping these green issues were given high priority in the manifestos of all major candidates.

To what extent, then, can it be argued that the work of select committees has contributed to this growth of public interest and the arrival of the environment on the policy agenda? The major reports discussed in this study, together with four more produced during the first two sessions of the 1987-92 parliament, had, over a concentrated period of six years, comprised an authoritative body of scientific fact and technologically advanced knowledge, a comprehensive lexicon of current understanding.

This persistent, long-term attention paid by the Environment Committee in particular to pollution and conservation issues was in some measure the cause of the prime minister's emphasis on environmental concerns in the 1988 series of speeches which culminated in the autumn in an address to the Conservative Party conference of that year, in which she said:

> We are not merely friends of the earth, we are its guardians and trustees. No generation has a freehold on this earth. All we have is a life tenancy - with a full repairing lease. This

government intends to meet the terms of that lease in full.
(Thatcher, 1988)

Despite some cynicism among commentators as to the genuineness
of this conversion, it can be traced in some detail to the series of
reports and their successors referred to above. Each of them brings
to bear the most recent scientific evidence and research results,
thoroughly explicated, combining the views of independent experts,
pressure groups and industry, as well as international opinion.
They amount, in sum, to a remarkable augmentation, if not to the
'greening' of public policy, then to explicit prime ministerial
support for a general policy emphasis which no one constituent in
the process would have achieved.

Is this, as some observers would say, simply a phase in policy
fashion: a convenient, populist bandwagon with which to deflect
more difficult issues or capture an initiative from opponents? If so,
then it may be no different from many other policy development
thrusts and will have the benefit of considered, authoritative and
comprehensive compilations from the select committees.

It is necessary now to itemise in detail the nature of the
influence which is brought to bear in this way; to construct a
'taxonomy of influence', based on the evidence and the case studies
accumulated in the previous pages and on what occurred
subsequently. By its nature such influence is often ambiguous,
sometimes minor or takes some time to emerge. It is not always
acknowledged and may occur in the deepest recesses of the
administrative machinery or the political system. This taxonomy is
confined to the evidence adduced from monitoring the work of
committees dealing with environmental policy issues, and does not
attempt to capture the work of other policy areas or select
committees. However, some attempt will be made in later pages to
consider the application of this concept to other areas of work.

The taxonomy contains the specific kinds of influence of which
examples abound in this study, but they should be supplemented by
the discernible and increasing stature which committees command
among ministers and departments, in the media and among those
who seek to influence the actions of Government.

Figure 13: A taxonomy of influence

Political context	The select committee's influence	Examples
The loophole in existing legislation	The committee investigation exposes the weaknesses in recent measures, showing that it has not covered all aspects of an issue or has been capable of being misused or avoided. The committee supports amending legislation.	HC 6 1984/85 HC 222 1988/89
New concerns brought to the attention of the House	Topics of a new, emergency or novel character such as acid rain and ozone layer on which action or new legislation is called for, are tabled in the House for the first time in substantive form.	HC 446 1983/84 HC 51 1985/86
Inadequacies of performance	The committee investigation exposes poor performance by a department or quango demonstrating that it is not fulfilling a legislative undertaking; or an Act designed to achieve a particular end is palpably not doing so; or an implementation programme is falling short of reasonable performance targets.	HC 414 1984/85 HC 101 1985/86 HC 562 1988/89
Administrative decision-making	The committee's scrutiny of actions, circulars and other administrative devices from departments produces new or improved procedures or a review of current practice. The committee exposes uncertainty or lack of clarity of administrative policy for the benefit of the policy community.	HC 275 1983/84 HC 414 1984/85

Political context	The select committee's influence	Examples
Eliciting facts, forecasts, projections from departments	The committee questions senior officials and ministers on the basis for their policy and action, testing their predictions, sharpening their assessments and examining the basis for legislative proposals by ministers.	HC 446 1983/84 HC 101 1985/86 HC 191 1985/86
Conflicts of policy	The committee investigation exposes conflicts between one department and another; conflicting policy objectives and contradictions in approach to issues.	HC 640 1983/84 HC 101 1985/86
Incorporating the quango	A collaborative approach between the committee and public utility or official body produces a change in Government policy or better resourcing for the benefit of the body concerned. The quango uses a committee enquiry to effect improvements in its funding, operating or status.	HC 146 1986/87 HC 446 1983/84
Updating available knowledge	In areas of rapidly advancing technology, the committee investigation provides a 'state-of-the-art' lexicon of scientific knowledge; challenges the supremacy of the department's scientists; establishes the limits of current research data.	HC 191 1985/86
Influencing the policy community	Committee reports, not always well received by Government, may have significant impact upon others in the policy community, modifying practice of other actors and achieving a contextual shift in the policy debate.	Chapter 10

Political context	The select committee's influence	Examples
Establishing new coalitions	The committee, acting as conduit for multiple interests, assists in establishing new collaborations or alliances between key actors both within and outside the parliamentary system, of a kind which did not exist before.	Chapter 10
Exposing interests	The committee process tends to ensure that the case being put by self-interest groups and lobbyists - especially those traditionally termed 'insider' groups - is exposed to the analysis of others, and especially to that of the 'outsiders' and issue-based lobby. The close relationships between industry and the official agencies such as NIREX or CEGB is exposed to public scrutiny.	HC 446 1983/84 HC 191 1985/86 Chapter 10
Mediation of interests	The investigative process can allow the committee to achieve some mediation between the interests of the self-interest groups and the ideological pressure groups.	Chapter 10
A bridge to Europe	The invitation by select committees to foreign governments and to the European Commission to give evidence or to comment on reports, and the committee's visits to polluted sites abroad, opens up channels of communication and creates linkages which enable other powers to put legislative strategies and policy plans directly to back-bench opinion, despite the resistance of the British Government.	Chapter 10 HC 51 1983/84 HC 22 1988/89

Political context	The select committee's influence	Examples
Raising the profile of issues	The fact of an aggressively-argued report registers an issue in the minds of MPs, the press and ministers, producing an increase in parliamentary questions, adjournment debates and ministerial comments.	Chapter 10 HC 446 1983/84 HC 6 1984/85 HC 191 1985/86
Assisting parliamentary specialisms	The persistent, long-term investigative activity of a committee such as that of the Environment Committee over three parliaments, into environmental pollution, creates a body of expertise and back-bench knowledge that ensures informed debate, incisive committee scrutiny of Bills and sharper debates on the floor, than would otherwise be possible.	Chapter 7
The spur to action	The attention of select committees produces action within departments, longer-term policy change, greater efficiency within quangos and in industry and opportunities for 'policy entrepreneurs' within the civil service, to promote policy development.	Chapter 10 HC 22 1988/89
Unacknowledged policy change	Many instances have been cited of committee recommendations being rejected in Government replies to reports, but with the appropriate policy change or action occurring subsequently without acknowledgement.	Chapter 10
Interest group accommodation	The committee performs the function of facilitating interest group accommodation and access, especially in the context where the Executive reduces its corporatist relationships (see Marsh, 1988).	Chapter 10

Committees have become a magnet for 'parliamentary consultants' and lobbyists of all kinds. Rush suggests that this is because they are in control of their agenda; perhaps also because they have the potential to set the political/policy agenda. They have the ability, through their reports to place information and advice on the public record in a form which carries the full legitimation of the House of Commons imprimatur (Rush, 1990; Grantham, 1989).

It remains true, as Drewry concludes, that the more exaggerated claims for select committee influence cannot be demonstrated in this taxonomy and that scrutiny and exposure rather than government or policy making are their real achievement. But Drewry also concedes that committees have grown in maturity since 1979/81. (Drewry, 1989, p 426) This study demonstrates that the boundary between scrutiny and policy change is by no means clear-cut. Much of the evidence here shows the contrary.

Departmentally linked committees have greatly extended their role in their first ten years. They have begun to scrutinise largely policy issues and the relationships with secretaries of state are developing ones. In the view of one 'insider', most ministers have tended increasingly to ensure that they carry the committee along with them and consequently committees have increased their influence with departments; they now acquire a good deal more information, both official and unofficial, than in the past (Cooper, 1987).

It is clear that committees have not consistently been a major force either of challenge to Executive actions or of alternative policy making; but they were never intended to be, as the above taxonomy demonstrates. However they have accepted the challenging role in a series of high-profile public disputes such as the Westland Helicopter affair, the salmonella in eggs scare and the financing of the National Health Service: two of which involved the resignation of ministers. It should be stressed that the immediate challenge to Government in these incidents was fought out in robust exchanges on the floor of the House; it was in the committee inquisition that the more painstaking sifting of issues was undertaken. In the highly-charged atmosphere of a censure debate it is easy for ministers to ride challenges, avoid questions and meet charge with counter-charge. Party discipline will ensure that votes are marshalled and the Government wins the day. It is all over in a few hours.

The real and lasting embarrassments to Executive high-handedness or cabinet disarray come with the all-party investigation: the detailed questioning of fact and motive, the more persistent media attention, the incremental revelations of the combatants, and even the refusal of Government witnesses to appear. All of these go to make the discomfiture of a minister in major political 'rows' of this kind more likely to be inflicted in a select committee than by the opposition front bench, and do more for the cause of open government.

Indeed, an active participant in the Defence Committee investigation into Westland Helicopters has recorded the view that it convinced the electronic media in particular of the news value of committees, but more importantly, "boosted their place in the constitutional firmament" (Gilbert, 1987). Drewry also believes this incident was a psychological landmark in the evolution of the committee system (Drewry, 1987).

Yet, for all the drama and impact which was created - most of it a long way from the Environment Committee - it can be argued that there were less spectacular but more important achievements. For example, the report which reviewed the options for replacing Polaris with a new strategic nuclear weapons system remains the best publicly-documented procurement ever made into nuclear weaponry (HC 36, 1981).

It will be necessary to return to the 'constitutional firmament' in later pages, to reflect upon the role of select committees in a constitutional context and to consider what functions they might perform, but there is consideration in the next section of whether the triangulation of issue type, mode and intervention as a basis for measuring influence has application in other policy areas.

The matrix approach: application to other policy areas

The matrix approach to measuring committee effectiveness, described in earlier chapters, has been tested on the reports in the environmental field of policy development. This section examines whether the salience of the technique has a broader application to other policy areas or to committees involved in quite different ranges of concern, and whether attempts by other select committees to evaluate their own performance have anything to teach the academic researcher.

As Drewry (1989, p 426) has commented, effectiveness has varied enormously from committee to committee. Many have remained on the sidelines of government. But it is possible to argue that he is too restrained in suggesting that select committees "must remain only in the business of scrutiny and exposure". In the environment policy area this book has shown direct policy change, legislative refinement and administrative modification. Is it not possible that in developing the increasingly significant role which Drewry acknowledges for other committees, he might find similar examples in other policy areas? At least two other select committees have given attention to the problems of assessing how far their recommendations have been taken up or have influenced Government thinking; and a third has taken a quite different approach to attempting to influence Government legislation.

The Trade and Industry Committee

In February 1988 the Trade and Industry Select Committee published a report which set out the fate of all the recommendations of its reports since 1980/81 (HC 343, 1988). It covered nine separate investigations, comprising 78 recommendations in all; each recommendation was followed by the Government's reply and the current position, together with a background note of the context. It shows that a substantial number of recommendations had been accepted, noted or at least welcomed, but as an approach to objective monitoring is perhaps flawed in that it relies entirely upon the DTI's own assessment, and their account of what progress or change had occurred subsequently. Even in the somewhat limited context of the fate of specific recommendations, it is less than adequate to rely on the department being monitored for an account of the impact made. Whilst it is reassuring to have the view of the department being monitored, this report would have carried more conviction if other actors had contributed to a rounded view of outcomes. Essentially HC 343 (1988) is a Government account or interpretation of committee performance, and for that reason of limited value.

The Social Services Committee

A more dynamic approach to this issue was provided by the Social Services Committee. Its chair, Frank Field, had said at an early stage:

> We are going to look at all our major reports, like those on community care and AIDS, and look at the progress on those fronts. We want to see whether the Government is responding to what the committee is saying and we want to look at the basis of those reports to see just how good the committee has been. (Field, 1988)

In fact, a comprehensive evaluation of that kind has not happened, mainly for lack of staff time, but there have been three papers from this committee which comprise a unique attempt to monitor its influence and at the same time to maximise its reports' effectiveness by intervening at the point of policy formation: that is to say, during the progress of Bills through the Commons, which relate directly to the policy under investigation.

In session 1983/84 the Social Services Committee produced a report entitled 'Children in care' examining policy concerning children looked after by local authorities, voluntary organisations and other bodies. The report made a number of recommendations including the setting up of a working party on childcare law (HC 360, 1984, paragraph 119).

The DHSS duly set up a working party and the subsequent White Paper led to the publication of the Children Bill. The response of the Social Services Committee was to produce a further report (HC 178, 1989) which sets out to examine the Children Bill in the light of the committee's 1983/84 report, to indicate to MPs which of the committee's recommendations the Government had accepted, partially accepted or rejected, and to comment on the provisions made.

HC 178 is therefore a handbook for MPs at each stage of the debate on the Bill, and potentially useful at the committee stage when clause by clause consideration is given. The document recommends acceptance or amendment of clauses and proposes to table amendments where necessary. All the professional and legal advice taken in evidence by the Social Services Committee was made available to back-bench MPs in their consideration of the detailed Bill. The committee is thus attempting to measure the efficacy of its original recommendations and to increase influence by intervening in the formulation of the legislation. In the terms used in this study it is an example of a committee intervention at the policy formulation stage in the policy cycle on a technical/legal issue. The effect of the committee mode and the outcomes established are outside our remit but make clear that the concepts employed can be translated to other contexts and to other committees.

The Social Services Committee utilised a similar technique in the 1989/90 session with two reports dealing with Government proposals for care in the community. The publication of the National Health Service and Community Care Bill which had been preceded by a White Paper in November 1989 prompted the Committee to produce a report in which it examined one immediate issue: the transitional arrangements for the funding of residential care for older people and other client groups in private and voluntary residential and nursing homes (HC 257, 1990). The committee evidence-taking sessions and the debates which they engendered were, therefore, synchronised with the progression of the Bill through parliament and again provided a sharply focused guide for parliamentarians in the major debates on the floor of the House on this topic. A second report (HC 277, 1989) undertook a similar exercise in regard to aspects of the funding of community care for local authorities.

The Energy Committee

The third example of this kind of action was that of the Energy Committee which intervened with a report on the privatisation of the electricity supply industry on a similar basis but at the stage when the Bill was in the House of Lords. This report (HC 307, 1988) provided their lordships with a side by side commentary on clauses under debate throughout the Bill.

Summary

Apart from these instances, however, there has been a demonstrable lack of interest on the part of most select committees to concern themselves with evaluating their effect on policy or the nature of their influence on Executive decision making or departmental administration.

Future students of select committees will, therefore, need to consider the robustness of the matrix approach promulgated above and to speculate with a judgement informed by both quantitative examination of outputs and a qualitative assessment of outcomes on its relevance to work in other policy areas. The following comments may be relevant.

First, the theoretical proposition that the degree of impact of the committee report may be related to the stage in the policy process that the subject matter has reached, is one which will have relevance to any area of policy under review. The research method employed here would allow analysis in that respect (see Figure 3, p 54) and would require students of select committees to relate the subject matter of recommendations to the process of policy development within the department being monitored. The 'agenda-setting' propensities of the committee can be differentiated from its evaluative role.

Second, in the examination of environmental policy we have categorised the investigations by issue type thus: technical/scientific; administrative; economic (see definitions Chapter 5). In the work of the other committees the categories might be quite different; for example, the subject matter might be predominantly legal, financial, social or indeed military or diplomatic. The principle, however, is valid that the nature of the issue or policy under review is relevant to the outcome and influence brought to bear.

Third, the mode of the committees investigation, here categorised in terms of the main thrust or tone of the investigative activity, in so far as its relevance to outcome has been demonstrated, will be equally of value in the areas of work of other departments. There is no reason to think that the outright challenge to the Executive will be any more successful in other departments of state than it is with ministers in the DOE.

It should be stressed again that by using the continuum acceptance-rejection of recommendations, only part of the picture is being examined; the nature of influence is far more subtle and less tangible than this quantitative analysis illustrates. It would still be essential, in measuring the success of committees operating in other policy areas, to elicit the qualitative impressions of key actors within those policy arenas.

The Procedure Committee review

It was in an attempt to capture this essentially evanescent quality of the select committee system that the Procedure Committee launched its own review of committee effectiveness, with a formal investigation started in November 1989. Ten years on from the introduction of the system, its witnesses gave just such a panoramic, impressionistic and self-critical examination of committee impact upon parliamentary affairs. In the next chapter there is a consideration of that review and of whether it has any bearing upon the formalistic structure of the matrix which has attempted to measure the environmental policy outcomes of the 1980s.

twelve

THE STORY SO FAR: A HOUSE OF COMMONS EVALUATION AND THE EMERGING CONSTITUTIONAL ISSUES

Introduction

This account of the Procedure Committee's evaluation makes clear that for those most closely involved in the activities of select committees - the back-bench MPs - the political priority is to ensure that progress is made at a pace which does not provoke Government hostility. Modest advances in structure and minor changes in practice are seen as the most effective means of capitalising on the progress of the first decade. There is no acknowledgement of the view propounded in this study that the future of the departmental select committee system is associated with the debate concerning modification of British constitutional practice or that it touches greatly on the need for procedural reform. In the following pages these issues are taken forward and an attempt is made to establish the constitutional limits to procedural reform, insofar as committee futures are concerned, and to contextualise the debate in a return to theoretical issues.

The first ten years

'The working of the select committee system' (HC 19, Session 1989/90) is the title of the Procedure Committee's review of the first ten years of the system. In a four month enquiry beginning in

December 1989 it examined all aspects of the work of departmental select committees and witnesses included committee chairs, the leader of the House, private members, officers of the House and pressure group representatives as well as academic commentators. There were 34 oral witnesses including 3 cabinet ministers. Eighty written memoranda from interested parties were supplemented by 14 detailed appendices.

The overall conclusions are that considerable success has been achieved in working across a wide range of issues and that the committee system represents a "far more vigorous, systematic and comprehensive scrutiny than anything that went before" (HC 19, 1990). A considerable number of the 70 recommendations are taken up with minor proposals for changes to standing orders and in some mild criticism of the failure of most committees to scrutinise expenditure adequately. The case is put for structural changes to enable science and technology policy to be covered by a new committee, and for health and social security departments to be monitored by separate select committees. A further recommendation argues for the law officer's department to come within the scrutiny system for the first time.

The report sees no imperative case for increasing powers of committees or for increasing staffing and resources. In examining the cost of committees, the powers to create sub-committees and the use of specialist advisers, members make somewhat hesitant and very modest proposals for change. The Procedure Committee sees no case for major change in the rules (the Osmotherly Rules) governing civil servants conduct in giving evidence, but pleads for a more open policy by the Government and more cooperation especially from the Treasury:

> We urge the Government to review its approach towards giving evidence with the aim of formulating a more constructive and open policy. (HC 19, 1990)

These recommendations amount essentially to some 'fine tuning' to the existing practice, summed up perhaps in recommendation xxvii: "we do not consider that new or additional powers for select committees are necessary or would be workable" (HC 19, 1990).

The pivotal evidence session was clearly that of the then leader of the House, Sir Geoffrey Howe. The Procedure Committee recognises that the continuous interplay between committees and departments and ministers is the most crucial and potentially sensitive of all the relationships which have to be maintained. Ministers and officials are the witnesses most frequently called; they share the main burden of scrutiny and they are the recipients of the great majority of committee recommendations. A somewhat critical tone might, therefore, have been expected in the evidence from the leader of the House. In fact the most striking feature of the Government's memorandum is a pragmatic acceptance of departmentally related committees as "an indispensable part of the work of the House of Commons". Sir Geoffrey drew upon four main illustrations of the value he placed upon the interaction of committees with Government. First, they provide "a ready and public platform for the Government to explain and describe its policies and the background to them". Second, he referred to the "testing of policy" by informed scrutiny and the knowledge that such scrutiny can always take place is a significant element in keeping departments performance to a high standard. Third, evidence from non-governmental sources was seen as a valuable contribution to the process of government and can "significantly influence and shape subsequent public debate" (HC 19, 1990). Fourth, in the view of the leader of the House, recommendations from select committees stimulate reconsideration of policy, whether or not proposals are actually accepted in the end.

These positive observations, however, were laced with minor concerns that committees should address themselves to topical subjects and be sharply focused if they were not to be overtaken by events. The additional workload placed upon ministers and officials was a difficulty in responding to requests for evidence from committees although Sir Geoffrey felt this could be a matter for negotiation. In some cases, he said, the process of policy formation could not be held back pending an investigation by a select committee.

There was general agreement amongst committees on the need for more debating opportunities and virtually all select committees regarded the present arrangements for debating their reports as inadequate. Committee chairs argued for a firmer link between the work of select committees and the House itself, regarding the present allocation of three estimates days for debating reports as entirely inadequate.

The Procedure Committee argued, however, that whilst understanding that a fixed quota of debates constitutes the umbilical cord linking committees to the work of the House, it nevertheless had doubts about whether such debates were taken seriously. It is, however, difficult, in the light of the evidence, to understand their recommendation on this point:

> On balance we do not recommend any increase in the three days currently available under the estimates day procedure. We are not persuaded that these debates and the limited attendance which they normally attract necessarily represent the best use of time on the floor of the House. (HC 19, 1990)

It went on to argue for a procedure whereby additional time might be made available for debating committee reports in some committee forum 'upstairs'.

One significant proposal, touching upon the resources available to select committees, is that there should be a limited availability of National Audit Office (NAO) staff and papers to committees pursuing topics which the Public Accounts Committee (PAC) have under investigation. This question is discussed in more detail later in this chapter, when the problems of a closer working relationship between the 'value-for-money' function and the wider scrutiny role are examined.

The report goes on to make the case that one of the main values of committee reports lies in their contribution to general debates on subjects to which they are relevant, sometimes forming the centrepiece of a wider discussion rather than being the subject of a substantive motion to approve or take note. The Procedure Committee does, however, confirm a number of other arguments pursued in this book; it commends the work of committees which persist in long-term themes, returning to earlier reports as the Environment Committee has done. It notes that the 'delayed drop' effect has wide application and that the links to the external and wider policy community are an important and relatively new element in the democratic process.

Indeed as this study has also demonstrated, pressure group involvement is acknowledged as central to the whole of the scrutinising function. Whether invited directly by a committee to give evidence or volunteering it, the report acknowledges that these groups all share the desire to influence, through their lobbying, the content of reports, the wider public debate and, ultimately, Government thinking.

For some academic commentators the failure to address the weaknesses in the Osmotherly Rules is a major defect. The committee noted that the rules have never been accepted by parliament but then, inexplicably, went on to argue that "a wholesale review at parliament's behest would simply result in a new set of guidelines which, while superficially less restrictive, would then be applied vigorously to the letter". They conclude: "At risk of defeatism therefore we believe that discretion is the sensible approach, particularly unless further experience demonstrates an urgent need for change" (HC 19, 1990).

That comment perhaps sums up the overall tone of this review of the first ten years and the attempt by one member, Graham Allen, to inject a more challenging stance into the report, to "breathe life, rights, independence and resources into parliament's most vital organs", was rejected on a division; the final report is in fact unanimous with a detectable flavour of self-satisfaction.

So whilst there seems to be a general consent to the overall success of the 1979 reforms, there is a noticeable gap in that the fundamental questions of the constitutional implications are virtually ignored. The committee limits itself to the comment that committees are not an alternative government, nor royal commissions producing detailed blue-prints for the future but, rather, provide more subtle and indirect impacts upon the course of events. In evidence, the architect of the 1979 reforms, now Lord St John, had set the tone when he suggested that the introduction of committees had left the constitutional principles underpinning the United Kingdom's system of government firmly in place and that it has never been the function of the House of Commons to govern but rather to be seen to check the Executive. He acknowledged the ambiguity of notions of 'check' and 'control' in this context, eschewing any suggestion of a radical shift in power from the Government to parliament.

It is, however, necessary for any detached observer to rehearse these underlying issues which arise and this chapter turns now to a closer look at what, if any, constitutional implications the existence of committees have, and in particular it makes an attempt to establish the constitutional limits to procedural reforms of this kind.

Constitutional reform or procedural change?

The scrutiny of the Executive and influence on its actions may be said to operate on a number of levels. The macro-level, at which parliament itself scrutinises Bills or the actions of ministers, works on the floor of the House and in procedural debates and question time, and in committee-stage proceedings.

At the other end of the spectrum, when the impact of policy or the action of civil servants affects individual citizens, MPs defend and promote the interests of their constituents. Whereas at the micro-level concern is likely to be with the practical details of policy, at the macro-level there will be a concentration upon principles and public policy (Bochel and Taylor-Gooby, 1988, p 209).

There is also, at a middle level of scrutiny, a range of activity in the work of royal commissions, committees of enquiry or judicial examinations, in which the distinction is not so clear. Matters of general policy cannot be entirely separated from particular cases and an enquiry into a specific incident will often carry an implication of scrutiny of a wider policy area.

Since 1979, with one or two notable exceptions, the setting up of royal commissions has been avoided, apparently on the personal preference of the then prime minister. Such bodies have, according to Hennessy, become "the most elevated and distinguished casualties of the Thatcher years" (Hennessy, 1985). Bochel and Taylor-Gooby (1988) argue that the growth of Government has adversely affected the ability of MPs in the 20th century to scrutinise and influence policy because of the sheer mass, specialism and complexity of the legislative programme and of Government activity. The environment, as has been shown, is one of the policy areas in which this trend has emerged, and it could be argued that in the absence of other mechanisms, the emergence of select committees has provided just such a device through which complex technical issues can be elucidated for the lay policy maker and those, both inside and outside Government, who will ultimately make policy or implement it. Sizewell and Windscale are examples of public enquiries which have left much doubt about the relationship of particular local issues to wider public policy (Layfield, 1987; Parker, 1978; Baker, 1988).

The select committee system has, among other things, deposited its members into the heart of these problems, creating a mechanism which, in the absence of other scrutinising devices, provides a stage upon which policy choice, scientific fact and political ideology meet, like the witches below Dunsinane. From the cauldron of the inquisitorial process come all-party committee reports attempting to clarify and make sense of ever more complex data and to monitor the Executive and its use, or misuse, of science in the justification of public policy.

Scrutiny, nevertheless, in the current political climate raises more basic considerations, particularly of the constitutional context of select committee activity. Conservative Governments of the 1980s have, in the view of many commentators, come to be perceived as centralist, de-regulating and, by some arguments, authoritarian. The combination of a large majority and fragmented opposition produced during this period a kind of demoralisation of the House of Commons. Bevins, for example, suggested there was a widespread feeling at Westminster and in Whitehall that Mrs Thatcher had mobilised her Commons majority to ram through legislation, scatter critics and crush the basic democratic power of parliament to amend; "the elective dictatorship has arrived" (Bevins, 1989).

In this atmosphere the select committees, in a number of notable examples, became the main focus of opposition, especially to some of the radical measures in the third term. Indeed, in a constitutional sense, apart from HM Opposition, select committees are one of the few structural means of achieving a countervailing force in these circumstances.

At the same time, the development of supra-national policy making in the EC requires not only procedural reform of the British parliament but a new look at the way parliament relates to the Community and how it tackles the growing volume of Community decision-making. Is there a case for the work of the European Scrutiny Committee, at the very least, to be supplemented by a more detailed examination of legislation by strengthened departmental committees? In this context John Biffen, lately leader of the House, comments: "the changing nature of Community membership makes Westminster procedural reform imperative; above all it is a Commons issue and should engage other loyalties besides those of party" (Biffen, 1989). And in the sense that the challenge is to parliament rather than to Executive, it is important that back-bench common cause is made: a role for select committees?

Graham and Prosser (1989) have argued that another tendency of the Thatcher Governments was to create an imposing edifice of quasi-government bodies, often replacing local government, in which traditional forms of democratic accountability are removed. UDCs, Joint Boards and HATs are examples. Whilst extended Government is by no means new, there have been no moves to design new forms of legitimating device or new institutions of accountability.

Under such conditions parliament no longer performs a critical, autonomous function of mediating between societal interests, being reduced, in Poggi's (1987) memorable phrase to "a highly visible stage on which are enacted vocal, ritualised confrontations between hierarchically controlled, ideologically characterised alignments". In the process of restoring the authority of the state whilst claiming to roll back its frontiers, there has been a weakening of the democratic underpinning which makes authority tolerable.

In a diffuse and uncoordinated debate about the need for constitutional reform, these underlying concerns have produced a variety of ideas. Wass has proposed a standing royal commission; Anthony Barker a standing constitutional commission; Hattersley has re-opened the devolution debate and Professor Crick has proposed a Bill of Rights. Walter Williams argues for wide-ranging procedural and administrative change which would emphasise the strategic planning role of the civil service and the cabinet office, with much less focus on the House and much more work done in committees with strengthened policy staffs.

The realistic position, however, is that there is no great pressure or crisis which might prompt a move to constitutional reform and in the two-party system upon which most parliamentary activity is premised, the role of other scrutinising mechanisms only comes into prominence when the Opposition is weak or the balance is held by other forces. When the two-party clash is at its fiercest and most direct, then the role of other scrutinising mechanisms reduces.

In this climate, the most likely development in the select committee system will be a modified procedural change, especially, as Biffen suggests, in the context of the need to come to terms with the growing volume of EC legislation and regulation.

In its report on this latter issue, the Procedure Committee (HC 622, 1989) proposes that more of the burden of debating proposed EC measures should move from the floor of the House to a series of five standing committees already available to the House under its standing orders. This proposal would involve giving the standing committees more power to examine in detail the legal, practical and policy implications of a proposal before going on to debate its merits on a substantive motion. This would involve more formal evidence taking in the manner of the special standing committees on Bills, but without usurping the powers of select committees to send for papers, persons and records.

It is, then, in this incremental mode of modest procedural development that the system of select committees will be likely to ground its own future growth.

The constitutional point to make is that whilst the introduction of select committees was part of a process of adjusting parliamentary structures for improving scrutiny of administration once it occurs, they are not as a rule (but with some notable exceptions) in a position to scrutinise or comment upon what is being put in place or proposed. What is needed is informed, effective input before legislation is passed.

There are, however, constitutional limits to procedural reform and the final pages of this study take the discussion forward to a consideration of the problems which such changes might face and how they might be introduced as an integral part of the development of the committee system.

thirteen

SUMMARY AND RECOMMENDATIONS

This final chapter considers what recommendations can be drawn from the case studies and from the subsequent development of committee activity, which would enable the present system to sharpen the scrutiny and monitoring of departments of state. These are recommendations not only to the parliamentary actors in the process but to other agents in the policy communities which committees address.

This study has argued that select committees have emerged as an important element in the constitutional pattern of scrutiny and monitoring of the Executive, different in type and style from HM Opposition in the role of calling Government to account. They are, perhaps paradoxically, more important in times when there is a powerful majority for the party in power and the Opposition is in retreat or in disarray, and they diminish in importance when the floor of the House assumes its full role as the theatre of ideological struggle in the two-party system. The study has also charted the development of committees as an important conduit for those outside Westminster to contribute to the process of pluralist policy formation.

Norton (1990) endorses this assessment of the first decade suggesting not only that departmental committees are now "the essential agents for scrutiny", but that they constitute the most significant parliamentary reform of the last eighty years: "the most important means of ensuring open government".

So much of the rhetoric in the debates which brought departmental select committees into being was about restoring balance between Executive and Legislature but our examination of a limited range of activity suggests that balances of a more subtle kind are also important. There is a balance to be struck between challenging or castigating departments and collaborating with them; between tough inquisition of ministers and an acceptance of their right to make policy; between partisan loyalty and all-party consensus. Balance too between interests and lobbies competing for the ear of policy makers; indeed it must be admitted that the one thing which committees have signally failed to do is overtly to restore more power to parliament at the expense of the Executive: it is not that kind of game.

McAuslan (1989) has highlighted the contrast between, on the one hand, increased parliamentary surveillance of the Executive and the administration as evidenced by the growth of select committees over the last decade, and on the other, a generally perceived drift during that period towards an authoritarian administration.

What then, does this study allow us to conclude?

Recommendations to the Right Honourable The House of Commons

The issue is the extent to which committees can extend their influence from monitoring and scrutiny and post-facto evaluation to a more effective and dynamic influence on primary legislation. In terms of the policy process model (Figure 3, p 54) they need, as a next step, to impact upon the early stages of the life-cycle of a policy.

1. There should be an acceptance that departmental committees look at all White Papers and Green Papers issuing from the departments they shadow; there should be a link to the existing process whereby the Committee on Statutory Instruments examines ministerial edicts before they are implemented.

Thus the emphasis would move from attempting to alter policy to helping to frame it. In this way when a standing committee came to give line by line consideration to a Bill, it might have before it a non-partisan appreciation of the Government's proposals. Earlier it was shown that the Social Services Committee made some attempt to do this in relation to the Children Bill and even tabled its own amendments.

The Procedure Committee's investigation (HC 19, 1990) into the first ten years of the departmental select committee system prompted all 14 committees to look - in some cases for the first time - at the fate of the recommendations they had made during their 10 year existence. Whilst one or two had previously made some attempt at this, most had not, and the crude totalling of acceptance/rejection is surprisingly favourable to the committees. But it prompts the almost obvious proposal that this audit of the fate of recommendations should be an established part of normal committee life.

2.   Committees should formally seek, once in each parliament, an account from their departments of what actions followed from acceptance of recommendations and what policy development, research outcomes or administrative changes were implemented in each case.

The decade of the 1980s, in which the departmental select committees were created and came to maturity, also saw the rebirth of interest in the evaluation and measurement of performance in public sector services. The development of the Management Information Systems for Ministers (MINIS) and the launch of the Financial Management Initiative (FMI) in 1982 were attempts to revive interest in the use of rational techniques of performance assessment and had the aim, in the words of Cmnd 9058 (on financial management in government departments), of assessing and wherever possible measuring outputs of performance in relation to stated objectives.

The complex issue of 'effectiveness' has to distinguish between administrative and policy effectiveness, however, something which, as Carter (1988, p 374) has argued, is not addressed fully in Treasury papers or in the Public Expenditure White Paper. Indeed the use of performance indicators seems not to have permeated the hearts and minds - the corporate culture - of many departments, mirroring what one key actor has termed a "lack of rigour" in the work of select committees who have lagged behind developments in management information techniques within departments (Garrett, 1990). There is an obvious area for closer scrutiny here, a fruitful field for monitoring performance which would suggest a more systematic approach by committees in the oversight of departments and agencies.

3.   One important role for select committees monitoring departments should be to examine the extent to which published measures of performance are utilised in established big spending programmes, and how far they are achieved.

The case studies have emphasised the evaluative role which committees can perform. It is a function which is better done outside the responsible department where entrenched interests and ministerial ideological priorities may cloud the outcome of policy evaluation studies. This point calls into question the clear stance taken by the Environment Committee under Sir Hugh Rossi as chair, who argued that his committee was likely to achieve more influence if it avoided topics of party political controversy which were likely to get aired in major debates in the House. This has, however, meant that the Environment Committee has not looked at any housing legislation since 1981. Throughout the 1980s there has been a series of radical measures from the DOE legislating major changes in the rights of tenants, the role of local authorities and the provision of social housing. This period has also seen a sharp decline in local authority house building, a large increase in homelessness, and the failure of the Housing Corporation and housing associations to meet targets or needs. By common consent there is a housing crisis. Why then does the Environment Committee not feel that its monitoring of the DOE should include these important structural shifts and, by most arguments, policy failure?

At the very least it should see an evaluation role and attempt to relate the legislative measures to service outcomes. Indeed it could be argued that the Housing Acts of 1985, 1988 and 1989 were fully thrashed out on the floor of the House of Commons and in the line by line committee stage. But these are essentially party political arenas - clashes of ideological stance - and in most cases have been abruptly ended by Government guillotine. They are no substitute for the painstaking inquisition of the committee enquiry. There is no opportunity to hear the local authorities and the tenants' groups, the independent experts or bodies such as the Institute of Housing or Shelter.

The analysis of the case studies demonstrates that scrutinising policy at the evaluation stage of its life cycle is the most fruitful point of intervention. Other committees would do well to follow the lead.

4. There should be a structured evaluation study in the programme of all select committees in which particular policies are formally assessed for effectiveness.

This of course has resource implications. Many contributors to the Procedure Committee assessment (HC 19) argued the need for more research and administrative staff for committees, and the chair of the Defence Committee especially drew attention to the problems posed by enquiries undertaken by the PAC and the staff of the NAO overlapping with those of other committees with minimal staff resources. The question needs to be asked whether the House of Commons is obtaining value for money from the outstanding resource which the NAO represents. In 1991 PAC was supported by 900 staff and £28 million a year budget. The remaining 13 departmental committees were supported by a total of 60 full-time staff and 80 part-time staff costing under £2 million a year.

This debate, however, has so far been premised on whether the departmental committees should be able to utilise the NAO material from their value-for-money investigations for PAC. There is a somewhat different point to be made.

From the case studies in this book it is clear that committees frequently make recommendations of a radical and far reaching nature, backed by analysis and research presented by their witnesses or independent experts and attested by specialist advisers. What they virtually never do is to provide sound estimates of the cost in capital and revenue expenditure that their recommendations imply. This is an important weakness especially in the areas of technological 'frontierism' which environmental policy explores, and undermines the intellectual excellence of many of the reports reviewed here. Committees need to concern themselves with the financial consequences of their recommendations.

This point reinforces a general reluctance by most select committees to take seriously that part of their brief which concerns departmental expenditure; a function reduced, in the case of the Environmental Committee, to a once-a-year superficial canter through departmental estimates.

5. To redress this weakness there should be an ability of committees to call upon the professional skills of the NAO and a commitment by the comptroller and auditor-general

(now an officer of the House), to service the reasonable
needs of the departmental committees.

This might require legislative change if he or she needs to address
other than value-for-money audits which he or she and the PAC
ordinarily undertake.

The impact which the select committee system has made, and
broadly acknowledged by the vast majority of those who gave
evidence to the Procedure Committee review (HC 19) is, however,
mainly appreciated by those who are involved in the process, policy
communities and pressure groups with whom they interact, and the
academic community who analyse their activities.

In the second decade of their existence it should be possible to
ensure that their public profile is raised and the undoubted growth
in media interest in their activities - enhanced by the introduction in
1989 of TV cameras and a weekly radio programme - is translated
into a wider public appreciation of their role.

6.   The reports that committees publish should be more widely
      available, better designed and a more conscious effort made
      to 'market' the meetings, publications and evidence sessions
      to the widest possible audience.

This might include the establishment of a press office, attractively
produced publications, bookstalls and a comprehensive approach to
marketing, with a deliberate attempt to attract media interest in
major reports and proposals, catching the attention of practitioners
within the policy community.

The limited number of occasions on which committee reports
are debated on substantive motions in the Commons is an issue to
be addressed. The link between committee corridors and the floor
of the House is tenuous, unstructured and intermittent.

7.   There should be a review of the arrangement for estimates
      day debates and a procedural entitlement to parliamentary
      prime time for debates on major committee reports when
      committees can report to the House on issues they believe
      are important.

In the first ten years of the select committee system the rules
governing the conduct of civil servants and departmental select
committees, and the limits of their ability to cooperate in

investigative probing, are laid down in a memorandum of guidance for officials appearing before select committees: the Osmotherly Rules. This document does not have statutory authority and in practice there have been few tensions between the demands of committee members and the limits imposed upon civil servants to answer questions. Those which have occurred, however, have been spectacular and are exemplified in the case of the Westland Helicopter issue of 1985. The attempts of both the Defence Select Committee and the Treasury and Civil Service Committee to investigate the issue were inhibited by a refusal by the Government to allow key civil servants to appear and to explain their conduct. Nor was the secretary to the cabinet willing, in his evidence, to name any individual involved or reveal what they had told him in his own enquiry into the incident.

In its response to these concerns the Government was categoric:

> The Government proposes to make it clear to civil servants giving evidence to select committees that they should not answer questions which are or appear to be directed to the conduct of themselves or other named individual civil servants. (Cm 78, 1987)

In distinguishing between 'conduct' and 'actions' of individual officials, the prime minister insisted that any suggestion of misconduct is a matter for the departmental minister concerned, and not for the select committee: "it is then for the minister to be responsible for informing the committee of what has happened."

This limitation is a major inhibition on the ability of a select committee to get to the core of issues such as that mentioned above and it is important that it is removed. Indeed on this and other subsequent occasions, ministers themselves have declined to cooperate fully in answering committee members questions, and it was in these circumstances that committees sent for officers.

8. The Government's guidelines for officials giving evidence should be withdrawn forthwith.

Apart from these occasional and high profile controversies the negative tone and 'ultra vires' ethos of the Osmotherly Rules seem no longer to be appropriate to real life activities on the committee corridor. There is an emerging consensus about the duties and accountability of public servants and it is also true that plans for the hiving-off of many functions of the civil service into new executive agencies, presaged in the Government's 'Next Steps' proposals, will mean that for those officials, an agreed basis of public accountability will have to be devised. A 1985/86 investigation by the Treasury and Civil Service Committee into the duties and responsibilities of ministers and civil servants echoed these concerns for revised practice to be established. The Single European Act is another reason for a rethink, since it will bring within the ambit of the British parliament a wide range of new administrative actions demanding accountability.

9.   The Osmotherly Rules should be redrafted into a simplified, short and much more positive code of conduct for civil servants, agents of public and executive agencies and staff of the EC, emphasising the need for maximum accountability and cooperation with committee enquiries and defining as narrowly as possible the areas of confidentiality and non-disclosure.

Recommendations to committee members

Given the intense political environment in which committees have to work there is an inevitable tendency for them to react to current crises and to exciting political issues of the day, but the evidence suggests that the greater value, in terms of positive response, will be in the longer-term issues and in persistence and depth of understanding.

An example is the long series of investigations conducted by the Environment Committee, now stretching over three parliaments and over a wide range of topics bearing on environmental policy. The progressive weight and build-up of scientific fact, new technological advance and updating of research findings is an important factor in the ultimate level of influence which the committee achieves on policy outcomes; it is perhaps a prime example of the value of continuity.

10.   The value of cumulative and persistent investigations in specific policy areas of a long period should be recognised by committees as an ingredient in exerting influence on policy outcomes, especially where Government policy is

developing incrementally, and where policy is at an 'evaluation' stage in the cycle.

This work would be enhanced if committees routinely commissioned evaluation studies from specialist consultants and research institutions to ensure thorough-going reviews, to include the pluralistic evaluation techniques touched upon in this work.

This study demonstrates that the mode in which a committee approaches an investigation will vary from an outright and aggressive challenge to a Governmental or departmental action, through to a collaborative and supportive attempt to help identify a policy response to a problem. The Westland Helicopter issue and the investigation into AIDS policy are recent examples outside the scope of this book, of the two extremes.

Whilst it is true that the challenging mode is rarely immediately productive of change, there is enough evidence on the 'delayed drop' phenomenon, to show that incremental change frequently results.

11. Committees should not fear that open challenge will be counter-productive and should recognise the importance of delayed outcomes, provided the quality of the report and its background research are soundly based.

The foregoing chapters have remarked on the dominant role played by the chair and the clerk in formulating the programme and topics investigated by committees. They are the essential 'gatekeepers' in the process perhaps to the detriment of other members and to the range of topics investigated. Sir Hugh Rossi's insistence on the avoidance of certain subjects is an example.

12. Members should influence the process more; they should ensure that there are no 'no-go' policy areas, implied or expressed, even if some issues are picked up at the evaluation stage, rather than at the formulation of policy.

This recommendation would be assisted if the whole procedure were more open and easily available to public scrutiny and there were some ability within the wider constituency of interests, to influence the direction of committee activity.

13.   Committees should publish more widely their sessional
       forward programmes of investigations.

Recommendations to those external to parliament

Earlier chapters have commented upon the frequency with which
certain issue-based pressure groups and large self-interest lobbies
are called to give evidence, whilst others with a less high public
profile do not become involved. This study has traced the way in
which some long-standing liaisons between groups and government
departments withered during the Thatcher years. Some have made
the transition to the committee corridor, others not.

14.   Generally interest groupings with a point to make need to be
       more keenly aware of the opportunity which the select
       committee system provides and to take a more proactive role
       in utilising the conduit which it establishes.

This constituency should be widened and a more catholic selection
of external groups should be enabled to be drawn into the process.
Reference to the tables of inputs and citations utilised in the matrix
in this research indicates that the evidence of pressure groups is a
substantial influence in committee reports. As one committee chair
commented: "We feel we are acting as a sounding board for people
who want to talk to the Government".

15.   Pressure groups should accept that select committees are a
       major new conduit for making representations to parliament
       and the executive, and should be utilised at every
       opportunity. They should note that the higher the quality of
       their submission the more likely it is that their case will be
       influential, especially in issues at the forefront of technical
       knowledge.

A number of witnesses to this research have commented adversely
on the contribution which local authorities have made to the select
committee process and to the quality of the evidence they have
supplied. As important partners in the implementation of much
public policy and the regulatory functions of the state - especially
in environmental policy, planning and conservation - there are

clearly advances to be made in exploiting the opportunities for dialogue and influence which committees provide.

16. The local authority associations and the major city and county authorities should make substantially more effort to register the interests and establish the importance of elected local democratic agencies in the formation of policy. They should give more attention to memoranda, research and evidence, utilising the vast body of data produced by the activities of councils to ensure that select committee enquiries are supplied with accurate and authoritative information essential to the process of policy mediation which committees seek to achieve.

There is a burgeoning interest from political scientists and the academic community in the progress of select committees as seen by the submission of evidence to the Procedure Committee enquiry (HC 19). The Study of Parliament Group has maintained a consistent monitoring of the progress they have made (Drewry et al, 1985; 1989).

This latter body has perhaps exhausted the benefits of the purely quantitative assessment of outputs and there needs now to be a basis for defining measurable elements as part of a qualitative emphasis on outcomes and a rather more prescriptive approach to defining best practice. The efficacy of the research method utilised here may have some bearing on the future of academic monitoring of the progress of committee system and especially on the approach to measuring 'success'.

17. The matrix approach and the triangulation of mode, issue type and intervention in the policy life-cycle may provide a sound basis for future research direction.

All groups, individuals and agencies with a professional or other practical interest in the policy area covered by a select committee investigation should recognise the potential value which may be contained in the investigative activities of the committee. Irrespective of the report's ability to directly influence Government policy, it may very well be a valuable compendium of developments in practice, a summary of the latest research data and an encyclopaedia of the latest thinking in the field under review.

Indeed, in the field of environmental conservation with which this book has been concerned, the imposition of standards is more likely to come from the EC than from the British Government. The evidence and research data provided by European officials may be more valuable as performance indicators than national targets.

18.   As in the example of the Social Services Committee's 1984/85 'Care in the community' report (not examined in detail in this study), reports may provide the whole policy community with a handbook or manual for the implementation of concepts not fully worked through in policy, budgetary or ministerial edicts from the Government department involved.

Concluding comment

As the reformed departmental select committees move into their second decade and the mother of parliaments approaches a new century and new links with Europe, the ability of back benchers to scrutinise and influence the Executive, be it a powerful and dominating one or one which balances the forces of a 'hung' parliament, is as important as it has ever been.   Modest development at a pace which 'keeps the mean between the two extremes of too much stiffness in refusing and too much easiness in admitting' the right of Governments to govern and right of parliament to demand redress, should ensure that the select committees consolidate the substantial, if undramatic, achievements sampled here: build upon the role that Norton (1990) has described as "the most important means of ensuring open government"; and give succour to the forces of pluralist democracy upon which the British state is based.

If the recommendations listed above, together with the far more extensive procedural proposals which came from the Procedure Committee review, are adopted, there is every chance that these modest objectives will be attained.

REFERENCES

Books, articles and interviews

Allaby, M. (1971) *The eco-activists: youth fights for the environment*, London: Charles Knight.

Allison, G. T. (1971) *Essence of decision*, Boston: Little and Brown.

Amery, L. (1951) *Thoughts on the constitution*, Oxford: Oxford University Press.

Bacharach, S. and Lawler, E. (1980) *Power and politics in organisations*, San Francisco: Jossey Bass.

Baker, R. (1988) 'Assessing complex technical issues: public inquiries or commissions', *Political Quarterly*, vol 59, no 2.

Barrett, S. (1989) Clerk to the Environment Committee in an interview with the author.

Bate, R. (1989) Senior planner of the Council for the Protection of Rural England in a letter to the author dated 22 August 1989.

Bell, N. (1988) Special adviser to the Environment Committee enquiry into acid rain (HC 446, 1984) in an interview with the author.

Bevins, A. (1989) 'What are MPs for?', *The Independent*, 1 March.

Biffen, J. (1984) 'The government's view', in D. Englefield (ed) *Commons select committees: catalysts for progress?*, Harlow: Longman.

Biffen, J. (1989) 'Time for the House to re-build its authority', *The Sunday Telegraph*.

Black, D. (1984) *Investigation of the possible increased incidence of cancer in west Cumbria*, Report of the Independent Advisory Group.

Blackstone, T. and Plowden, W. (1980) 'Dear Mr Ibbs', *The Observer*, Sunday 6 April.

Blowers, A. (1987) 'Transition or transformation? - environmental policy under Thatcher', *Public Administration*, vol 65, no 3.

Bochel, H. and Taylor-Gooby P. (1988) 'MPs influence on welfare policy', *Parliamentary Affairs*, vol 41, no 2.

Brookes, S. K., Jordan, A. G., Kimber R. H. and Richardson J. J. (1976) 'The growth of the environment as a political issue in Britain', *British Journal of Political Science*, no 6, pp 245-55.

Burch, M. and Wood, B. (1983) *Public policy in Britain*, Oxford: Martin Robertson.

Burgess, R. G. (1982) *Field research: a source book*, Boston: George Allen and Unwin.

Butt, R. (1969) *The power of parliament*, London: Constable.

Carter, N. (1988) 'Measuring government performance', *Political Quarterly*, vol 59, p 369.

Cawson, A. (1982) *Corporatism and welfare*, London: Heinemann.

Central Electricity Generating Board (1984) *Evidence to the Environment Select Committee*, 21 May, (in HC 446 II), London: HMSO.

Cheshire County Council (1983) *Memorandum submitted to Select Committee on the Environment*, (published as appendix to report HC 275-III), London: HMSO.

Churchill, Sir W. (1930) *Parliamentary government and the economic problem*, Oxford: Clarendon/OUP.

Coombes, D. (1966) *The member of parliament and the administration*, London: Allen and Unwin.

Cooper, Sir F. (1987) 'A view from a witness', *Contemporary Record*, vol 1, no 1.

Council for Protection of Rural England (1984) *Evidence to the Environment Select Committee*, 7 November, (in HC 6), London: HMSO.

Craigen, J. (1984) 'The backbenchers view' in D. Englefield (ed) *Commons select committees: catalysts for progress?*, Harlow: Longman.

Crick, B. (1965) *The reform of parliament*, London: Anchor Books.

Deakin, N. (ed) (1986) *Policy change in government*, London: Royal Institute of Public Administration.

Dobson, M. (1984) 'Seminar report on green belts and housing', *The Planner*, February.

Drewry, G. (1985) 'Scenes from committee life' in G. Drewry (ed) *The new select committees*, Oxford: Oxford University Press.

Drewry, G. (1987) 'The Defence Committee on Westland', *Political Quarterly*, vol 58, no 1.

Drewry, G. (ed) (1989) *The new select committees*, 2nd edition, Oxford: Clarendon Press.

Dror, Y. (1973) *Public policymaking re-examined*, Aylesbury: Leonard Hill.

Du Cann, E. (1981) 'Parliament, select committees and democracy', *Public Money*, vol 1, no 1.

Du Cann, E. (1984) 'The chairman's view' in D. Englefield (ed) *Commons select committees: catalysts for progress?*, Harlow: Longman.

Easton, D. (1965) *A systems analysis of political life*, New York: Wiley.

Emery, Sir P. (1989) Chairman of the Procedure Committee, quoted in *The Independent*, 20 February.

Etzioni, A. (1964) *Modern organisations*, New Jersey: Prentice-Hall.

Field, F. (1988) 'The thoughts of Chairman Field', *Community Care*, 4 February.

Friends of the Earth (1984) *Friends of the Earth Evidence to Environment Select Committee*, 23 May, (in HC 446 II), London: HMSO.

Foot, M. (1976) *Evidence to the Select Committee on procedure*, (in HC 588), London: HMSO.

Foot, M. (1979) Speech reported in *Hansard Weekly Edition*, 20 February, London: HMSO.

Forestry Commission (1984) *Evidence to the Environment Select Committee*, 25 June, (in HC 446 II), London: HMSO.

Forrester, J. W. (1971) *World dynamics*, Cambridge, Mass: The Wright-Allen Press.

Garrett, T. M. P. (1990) *Evidence to the Procedure Committee*, (in HC 19 xiii), London: HMSO.

Giddings, P. (1985) 'What has been achieved?' in Drewry (ed) *The new select committees*, Oxford: Oxford University Press.

Gilbert, Dr J. (1987) 'Grand inquisitor', *Contemporary Record*, vol 1, no 1.

Golding, J. (1984) 'The chairman's view II' in D. Englefield (ed) *Commons select committees: catalysts for progress?*, Harlow: Longman.

Graham, C. and Prosser T. (1989) 'The constitution and the new Conservatives', *Parliamentary Affairs*, vol 42, no 3.

Grant, Dr M. (1988) The special adviser to the Environment Committee enquiry into planning: appeals, call-in and major public enquiries, HC 181 Session 1985/6, in an interview with the author.

Grantham, C. (1989) 'Parliament and political consultants', *Parliamentary Affairs*, vol 42, no 4.

Greenpeace (1988) In correspondence with the author.

Gregory, R. (1971) *The price of amenity*, London: Macmillan.

Gren, A. (1987) Clerk to the Environment Committee in an interview with the author.

Griffith, P. (1985) 'A party political role for select committees', *London Review of Public Administration*, no 17, Royal Institute of Public Administration.

Hailsham, Lord (1976) The Dimbleby Lecture, published in *The Listener*, 21 October.

Haldane, Lord (1918) *The machinery of government*, (in Cd 9230), London: HMSO.

Hall, D. (1983) 'Tightening the green belt', *Town and Country Planning*, vol 52, no 10.

Ham, C. and Hill, M. (1984) *The policy process in the modern capitalist state*, Brighton: Wheatsheaf.

Hamilton, W. (1979) Speech reported in *Hansard Weekly Edition*, 25 June, London: HMSO.

Hawkins, R. (1989) 'Talking tough on toxic waste', *Surveyor*, 23 March.

Hayward, J. and Norton, P. (1986) *The political science of British politics*, Brighton: Wheatsheaf.

Hennessy, P. (1985) 'The good and the great', *The Listener*, vol 213, no 2895, 7 February.

Hennessy, P. (1989) 'Whitehall watch', *The Independent* 20 February.

Hill, A. and Whichelow, A. (1964) *What's wrong with parliament*, London: Penguin.

Hill, D. (ed) (1984) *Parliamentary select committees in action: a symposium*, Strathclyde University paper no 24, Glasgow: Strathclyde University.

Hogwood, B. (1987) *From crisis to complacency: shaping public policy in Britain*, Oxford: Oxford University Press.

Hogwood, B. and Gunn, L. (1984) *Policy analysis for the real world*, Oxford: Oxford University Press.

House Builders Federation (1989) A spokesperson of the House Builders Federation in an interview with the author.

Irwin, H. (1988) Clerk to the Social Services Select Committee in a conversation with the author.

Jenkin, P. (1983) Speech to the summer school of the Royal Town Planning Institute, published in *The Planner*, February 1984.

Jenkins, B. and Gray, A. (1983) 'Bureaucratic politics and power', *Political Studies*, vol 31, no 2.

Jenkins, W. I. (1988) Review article in *Public Administration*, vol 66, no 1.

Johnson, N. (1966) *Parliament and administration*, London: Allen and Unwin.

Johnson, N. (1984) 'The academics view' in D. Englefield (ed) *Commons select committees: catalysts for progress?*, Harlow: Longman.

Johnson, N. (1988) 'Departmental select committees' in M. Ryle and P. Richards (eds), *The Commons under scrutiny*, London: Routledge.

Jones, G. W. (1984) 'The House of Commons - a threat to good government', *London Review of Public Administration*, no 16, Royal Institute of Public Administration.

Jones, Dr R. R. (1988) Speech to the International Conference of Environmental Scientists, 29 November 1988, London.

Jordan, A. and Richardson J. J. (1989) *Government and pressure groups in Britain,* London: Clarendon Press.

Judge, D. (1983) *The politics of parliamentary reform*, London: Heinemann.

Judge, D. (1990) (in press)

Kaufman, G. (1979) Speech reported in *Hansard Weekly*, 25 June, London: HMSO.

Lankester, R. S. (1980) 'House of Commons select committees related to government departments', *The Table*, vol 48.

Laski, H. (1920) *A grammar of politics*, London: Allen and Unwin.

Layfield, Sir F. (1987) *Report of the public enquiry into the Sizewell 'B' Nuclear Power Station*, London: HMSO.

Lindblom, C. E. (1959) 'The science of muddling through', *Public Administration Review*, no 19, pp 517-26.

Lindblom, C. E. (ed) (1980) *The policy-making process*, New Jersey: Prentice Hall.

Lock, G. (1985) 'Resources and operations of committees' in G. Drewry (ed) *The new select committees*, Oxford: Oxford University Press.

Mackintosh, J. (1969) in *The Times*, 13 March.

Marsh, D. (ed) (1983) *Pressure politics*, London: Junction Books.

Marsh, I. (1986) *Policy making in a three party system*, London: Methuen.

McAuslan, P. (1989) 'Parliamentary control of the administrative process', *Political Quarterly*, vol 60, no 4.

Middlemass, K. (1979) *Politics in industrial society*, London: Deutsch.

Miles, M. and Huberman, A. (1985) *Qualitative data analysis*, London: Sage.

Ministry of Housing and Local Government (1955) *Green belts*, Circular 42/55 3 August, London: HMSO.

Moran, M. (1985) *Politics and society in Britain*, London: Macmillan.

Morris, C. (1984) 'The opposition's view' in D. Englefield (ed) *Commons select committees: catalysts for progress?*, Harlow: Longman.

Nature Conservancy Council (1984) *Evidence to the Environment Select Committee*, 12 November, (in HC 6), London: HMSO.

Nixon, J. and Nixon, N. (1983) 'The Social Services Committee', *Journal of Social Policy*, vol 12, no 3.

Norton, P. (1983) 'The Norton view ' in D. Judge (ed) *The politics of parliamentary reform*, London: Heinemann.

Norton, P. (1990) *Evidence to the Procedure Committee*, (in HC 19 viii), London: HMSO.

Palmer, A. (1968) *Hansard*, 23 May, London: HMSO.

Palmer, V. (1928) *Field studies in sociology: a students manual*, Chicago: University of Chicago Press.

Parker, Mr Justice (1978) *The Windscale enquiry*, London: HMSO.

Patterson, W. (1988) The Special Adviser to the Environment Committee enquiry into radioactive waste (HC 191 1985/6) in an interview with the author

Pfeffer, J. (1981) *Power in organisations*, Mass: Pitman.

Poggi, G. (1987) *The development of the modern state*, London: Hutchinson,

Porritt, J. (1988) Quoted in *The Sunday Telegraph*, 4 December.

Potter, A. (1961) *Organised groups in British national politics*, London: Faber.

Powell, E. (1979) Speech reported in *Hansard Weekly*, 25 June, London: HMSO.

Price, C. (1984) 'Making a select committee work', *Public Money*, March.

Pym, F. (1978) Speech to the Cambridge University Conservative Association, Conservative Central Office, London.

Pym, F. (1987) 'Origins of the new select committees', *Contemporary Record*, vol 1, no 1.

Redlich, J. and Ilbert, C. (1908) *Procedure of the House of Commons*, vol II, London.

Reiners, W. J. (1985) 'The Environment Committee' in G. Drewry (ed) *The new select committees*, Oxford: Oxford University Press.

Rhodes, R. A. W. (1981) *Control and power in central local government relations*, London: Gower.

Richardson, J. and Jordan, A. (1979) *Governing under pressure*, Oxford: Martin Robertson.

Richardson, J. and Jordan, A. (1984) 'Evidence to parliamentary committees as access to the policy process' in D. Hill (ed) *Parliamentary select committees in action: a symposium*, Strathclyde University paper no 24, Glasgow: Strathclyde University.

Rivers, P. (1974) *Politics by pressure*, London: Harrap.

Robinson, A. (1978) *Parliament and public spending*, London: Heinemann.

Robinson, A. (1985) 'The financial work of select committees' in G. Drewry (ed) *The new select committees*, Oxford: Oxford University Press.

Rossi, Sir H (1985a) *First Report of the Liaison Committee*, (in HC 363), London: HMSO.

Rossi, Sir H. (1985b) *Report of the Environment Select Committee*, (in HC 446 I), London: HMSO.

Rossi, Sir H. (1987) In an interview with the author.

Rossi, Sir H. (1988) In the preface to the *First report of the Environment Committee*, (in HC 270 I), London: HMSO.

Rossi, Sir H. (1989a) *Toxic waste: The second report of the Environment Committee*, Session 1988/9, vol 1, London: HMSO.

Rossi Sir H (1989b) Chairman of the Environment Committee interviewed on the BBC programme *In Committee*, 12 March.

Royal Town Planning Institute (1984) *Evidence to the Select Committee on Environment*, (in HC 275 viii), London: HMSO.

Royal Society for the Protection of Birds (1984) *Evidence to the Environment Select Committee*, 26 November, (in HC 6), London: HMSO.

Rush, M. (1990) 'Select committees', in M. Rush (ed) *Parliament and pressure politics*, Oxford: Oxford University Press.

Ryle, M. and Richards, G. (1988) *The Commons under scrutiny*, London: Routledge.

Schmitter, P. (ed) (1979) *Trends towards corporatist intermediation*, London: Sage.

Sedgemore, B. (1980) *The secret constitution*, London: Hodder and Stoughton.

Shell, D. (1970) 'Specialist select committees', *Parliamentary Affairs*, vol XXIII.

Simon, H. (1958) *Administrative behaviour*, New York: Macmillan.

Smith, G and Cantley, C. (1985) *Assessing health care: a study*, Milton Keynes: Open University Press.

Smith, L. M. (1978) 'An evolving logic of participant observation and other case studies' in Shulman (ed) *Review of research in Education*, vol 6, Illinois: Peacock.

Stevas, N. St. J. (1979) HC Debates, vol 969, 25 June, *Hansard*, London: HMSO.

Stewart, J. D. (1958) *British pressure groups*, Oxford: Clarendon Press.

Stringer, J. K. and Richardson, J. J.(1980) 'Managing the political agenda: problem definition in policy-making in Britain', *Parliamentary Affairs*, no 23, p 23-29.

Thatcher, M. (1988) Speech to the Conservative Party Conference, Brighton, October, London: Conservative Central Office.

The Economist (1977) Editorial comment, 5 November.

The Times (1983) Editorial comment, 8 August.

Waldegrave, W. (1984) Letter to Trade and Industry Committee dated 16 July, (in HC 640), London: HMSO.

Walkland, S. (1976) 'The politics of parliamentary reform', *Parliamentary Affairs*, vol XXIX.

Walkland, S. (1985) Foreword to G. Drewry (ed) *The new select committees*, Oxford: Oxford University Press.

Warren Spring (1984) *Evidence of the Warren Spring Laboratory to the Environment Select Committee*, 13 June, (in HC 446 II), London: HMSO.

Wass, D. (1984) 'Government and the governed', in *1983 BBC Reith Lectures*, London: Routledge and Kegan Paul.

Webb, S and Webb, B. (1920) *A constitution for the socialist commonwealth of Great Britain*, (Reprinted 1975) Cambridge: Cambridge University Press.

Weatherill, B. (1984) Foreword to D. Englefield (ed) *Commons select committees: catalysts for progress?*, Harlow: Longman.

Winkler, J. T. (1974) 'The coming corporatism', *New Society*, 19 October.

Wintour, C. (1988) in *The Times*, 6 September.

Official papers and government documents

Cm 43 (1986) *The Government's response to the fifth report of the Environment Committee*, Session 1985/86, London: HMSO.

Cm 78 (1987) *Accountability of ministers and civil servants*, Session 1986/87, London: HMSO.

Cm 679 (1989) *The Government's response to the second report of the Environment Committee*, Session 1988/89, London: HMSO.

Cmnd 9058 (1983) *Financial management in government departments*, London: HMSO.

Cmnd 9397 (1984) *Acid rain: the Government's reply to the fourth report of the Environment Committee*, Session 1984/85, London: HMSO.

Cmnd 9522 (1985) *Operation and effectiveness of Part II of the Wildlife and Countryside Act: the government's reply to the first report of the Environment Committee*, Session 1984/85, London: HMSO.

Cmnd 9852 (1986) *Radioactive waste: the Government's response to the Environment Committee's Report*, London: HMSO.

Department of the Environment (1983) *Financial guidance for management agreements*, Circular 4/83, London: HMSO.

Department of the Environment (1984a) *Evidence to Environment Select Committee*, 11 June, (in HC 446 II), London: HMSO.

Department of the Environment (1984b) *Green belts*, Circular 14/84 and *Land for housing*, Circular 15/84, 4 July, London: HMSO.

Hansard (1976) *House of Commons Official Report*, 2 February, London: HMSO.

Hansard (1979a) *House of Commons Official Report*, 19-20 February, London: HMSO.

Hansard (1979b) *House of Commons Official Report*, 25 June, London: HMSO.

Hansard (1981) *House of Commons Official Report*, 27 April, London: HMSO.

Hansard (1984) Appendix to the weekly report, vol 63, no 185, col 161/2, London: HMSO.

HC 6 (1984) *First Report of the Environment Committee*, Session 1984/85 vols I/II London: HMSO.

HC 19 (1990) *The working of the select committee system: second report of the Procedure Committee*, Session 1989/90, vol 1, London: HMSO.

HC 22 (1989) *Toxic waste: the second report of the Environment Committee*, Session 1988/89, London: HMSO.

HC 36 (1981) *Strategic nuclear weapons policy: fourth report of the Defence Committee*, Session 1980/81, London: HMSO.

HC 51 (1986) *First special report of the Environment Select Committee: acid rain* (follow-up), Session 1985/86, London: HMSO.

HC 62 (1986) *First report of the Treasury and Civil Service Committee: minister and civil servants*, Session 1986/87, London: HMSO.

HC 100 (1986) *First report of the Liaison Committee: accountability of ministers and civil servants*, Session 1986/87, London: HMSO.

HC 101 (1985) *First report of the Committee on Welsh Affairs: coastal sewage pollution in Wales*, Session 1985/86, vols I and II, London: HMSO.

HC 146 (1986/87) *Historic buildings and ancient monuments: the first report of the Environment Select Committee*, vol II Session 1986/87, London: HMSO.

HC 178 (1989) *Children Bill: second report of the Social Services Committee*, Session 1988/89, London: HMSO.

HC 181 (1986) *Planning: appeals, call-in and major public enquiries: the fifth report of the Environment Committee*, Session 1985/86, vol 1, London: HMSO.

HC 183 (1987) *Pollution of rivers and estuaries: third report of the Environment Committee*, Session 1986/87, London: HMSO.

HC 191 (1986) *Radioactive waste: first report of the Environment Committee*, Session 1985/86, vol II, London: HMSO.

HC 257 (1990) *Community care: future funding of private and residential care: second report of the Social Services Committee*, Session 1989/90, London: HMSO.

HC 268 (1988) *The government's observations on the first report of the Environment Committee*, (HC 146 1986/87), Session 1987/8, London: HMSO.

HC 270 (1988) *Air pollution: the first report of the Environment Committee*, Session 1987/88, London: HMSO.

HC 275 (1984) *Green belt and land for housing: first report of the Environment Committee*, Session 1983/84, London: HMSO.

HC 277 (1990) *Community care: funding for local authorities: third report of the Social Services Committee*, Session 1989/90, London: HMSO.

HC 303 (1965) *Fourth report of the Procedure Committee*, Session 1964/65, London: HMSO.

HC 307 (1988) *Structure, regulation and economic consequences of electricity supply in the private sector: third report of the Energy Committee*, Session 1987/88, London: HMSO.

HC 321 (1985) *The government's response to the 'the wealth of waste': the fourth report of the Trade and Industry Committee* (1983/4), Session 1984/85, London: HMSO.

HC 343 (1988) *Monitoring the Department of Trade and Industry: first special report of the Trade and Industry Committee*, Session 1987/88, London: HMSO.

HC 360 (1984) *Children in care: second report of the Social Services Committee*, Session 1983/84, London: HMSO.

HC 363 (1985) *First report of the Liaison Committee*, Session 1984/85, London: HMSO.

HC 414 (1985) *Third report of the Environment Committee*, Session 1984/85, London: HMSO.

HC 446 (1984) *Fourth report of the Environment Committee*, Session 1983/84, vols I/II, London: HMSO.

HC 446-II (1984) *Acid rain: the fourth report of the Environment Select Committee*, vol II, Session 1983/84, London: HMSO.

HC 543 (1988) *Pollution of rivers and estuaries: third special report of the Environment Committee*, Session 1987/88, London: HMSO.

HC 588 (1978) *Report of the Procedure Committee*, Session 1977/88, London: HMSO.

HC 622-1 (1989) *Fourth report of the Procedure Committee*, Session 1989/90, on the scrutiny of European legislation, London: HMSO.

HC 635 (1984) *The fifth special report of the Environment Committee*, Session 1983/84, London: HMSO.

HC 640 (1984) *The wealth of waste: the fourth report of the Trade and Industry Select Committee*, Session 1983/84, London: HMSO.

INDEX

INDEX

Index compiled by Ann Barham